T0181977

Introduction to Unity ML-Agents

Understand the Interplay of Neural Networks and Simulation Space Using the Unity ML-Agents Package

Dylan Engelbrecht

Apress®

Introduction to Unity ML-Agents: Understand the Interplay of Neural Networks and Simulation Space Using the Unity ML-Agents Package

Dylan Engelbrecht
Cape Town, South Africa

ISBN-13 (pbk): 978-1-4842-8997-6   ISBN-13 (electronic): 978-1-4842-8998-3
https://doi.org/10.1007/978-1-4842-8998-3

Managing Director, Apress Media LLC: Welmoed Spahr
Acquisitions Editor: Spandana Chatterjee
Development Editor: Spandana Chatterjee
Coordinating Editor: Mark Powers

Cover designed by eStudioCalamar

Cover image by Deepmind on Unsplash (www.unsplash.com)

Distributed to the book trade worldwide by Apress Media, LLC, 1 New York Plaza, New York, NY 10004, U.S.A. Phone 1-800-SPRINGER, fax (201) 348-4505, e-mail orders-ny@springer-sbm.com, or visit www.springeronline.com. Apress Media, LLC is a California LLC and the sole member (owner) is Springer Science + Business Media Finance Inc (SSBM Finance Inc). SSBM Finance Inc is a **Delaware** corporation.

For information on translations, please e-mail booktranslations@springernature.com; for reprint, paperback, or audio rights, please e-mail bookpermissions@springernature.com.

Apress titles may be purchased in bulk for academic, corporate, or promotional use. eBook versions and licenses are also available for most titles. For more information, reference our Print and eBook Bulk Sales web page at http://www.apress.com/bulk-sales.

Any source code or other supplementary material referenced by the author in this book is available to readers on GitHub (https://github.com/Apress). For more detailed information, please visit http://www.apress.com/source-code.

Printed on acid-free paper

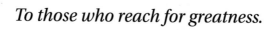

To those who reach for greatness.

Table of Contents

About the Author ....**xi**

About the Technical Reviewers ....**xiii**

Acknowledgments ....**xv**

Introduction ....**xvii**

Chapter 1: Introduction...1

What Is Machine Learning?..1

How We Use Machine Learning in the Modern Day.............................2

Prerequisites...5

Conclusion 6

Chapter 2: History of AI and Where We Are Today 7

The People Who Shaped Artificial Intelligence.................................7

Alan Mathison Turing..8

John McCarthy 8

Marvin Lee Minsky 9

Guido van Rossum 9

Modern-Day Companies Paving the Future of AI 9

Python Software Foundation 9

Nvidia 10

IBM 11

Google 11

Tesla 12

OpenAI 13

How AI Has Evolved in Games, from Chess to *Dota 2* 14

   So, Where Are We Now with AI in Game Development? 14

Conclusion 17

Chapter 3: The Future of AI and Ethical Implications 19

The Future of AI 20

   Law and Justice 20

   Healthcare 21

   Taxes and Governance 22

   Life Extension and Brain-Computer Interfaces 23

   Entertainment 24

Avoiding a Bad Future 25

Bias and Why We Need Diverse Datasets 26

   So, What Is Bias in AI? 26

   Why We Need Diverse Datasets 26

Discussing the Moral and Ethical Implications 27

Why AI? 28

Flavors of AI 28

AI Road Map and Classification 29

   Reactive Machines 31

   Limited Memory 32

   Theory of Mind 33

   Self-Aware 34

Machine Learning with Unity ML-Agents 36

   Reinforcement Learning 37

   Imitation Learning 39

   Neuroevolution 40

Practical Use Cases for Unity ML-Agents...40

Learning How to Build Machine Learning Agents..41

Self-Driving Cars 41

Game AI 41

Robotics...42

Simulated Space for Agent Training 43

Training Gym for Agents 44

Conclusion 44

Chapter 4: Dopamine for Machines 47

Dopamine...48

Dopamine in Humans 48

Dopamine in Animals...50

Dopamine in Machines 50

Training Reinforcement Learning Agents...53

How and When to Reward Your ML-Agents 54

A Sound Reward System Makes for Great ML-Agents 56

How Reward Systems Influence Training Time...57

Various Aspects of Rewarding and Punishing ML-Agents...58

Team-Based Rewards...59

Conclusion...60

Chapter 5: ML-Agents Setup...61

Unity Setup...61

New Project Setup...62

ML-Agents Unity Package Setup...63

Installing the ML-Agents Extensions Package...65

Opening the Example GitHub Project...66

Python Setup...75

    Creating a Virtual Environment...78

    Installing ML-Agents and Dependencies...............................81

Validating Our ML-Agents Installation with Samples............83

Conclusion 85

Chapter 6: Unity ML-Agents..87

ML-Agent Components 87

    Behavior Parameters 89

    The Decision Requester...93

Learning Environments 94

    The Agent 96

Inputs and Outputs...102

    Inputs, Observations, and Sensors 102

Actions 122

    Continuous...123

    Discrete 124

Heuristics..126

Rewards..126

Training an Agent 129

Conclusion 134

Chapter 7: Creating Your First AI in Unity 137

Planning an Agent...138

The Avoidance Sample..138

    Reward Scheme 139

    Observation Plans...142

Actions Planning..142

Expected Challenges 143

Building Your First ML-Agent 144

The Grid Sensor..156

The Ray Perception Sensor 161

Building the Environment..165

Understanding Hyperparameters...167

Training Your Agent 170

Duplicating Your Training Zones 171

TensorBoard and Why It's Essential for Training.............................172

Connecting Stand-Alone Builds to Python.......................................174

Exporting and Loading Your Model 176

Conclusion 176

Chapter 8: Solve a Challenge with AI 179

The Challenge 179

Grazer Agents 180

Predator Agents 180

Bonus Objective..180

Before You Start..181

Other Techniques to Consider 181

CL (Curriculum Learning)..182

BC (Behavioral Cloning) 186

Self-Play 187

Tips 189

Conclusion 190

Chapter 9: Next Steps **191**

   Explore 191

      Additional ML-Agent Functionality 191

      Documentation 192

   Conclusion 193

Index..**195**

About the Author

Dylan Engelbrecht is a seasoned gameplay engineer and author of *Building Multiplayer Games in Unity: Using Mirror Networking*.

He is an avid gamer who loves immersive experiences and real-time strategy games. He has worked for top enterprise and commercial game development studios in Africa, with several games under his belt: *A Township Tale, Gorn, A Memoir Blue,* and others.

About the Technical Reviewers

Simon Jackson is a long-time software engineer and architect with many years of Unity game development experience, as well as an author of several Unity game development titles. He loves to both create Unity projects as well as lend a hand to help educate others, whether it's via a blog, vlog, user group, or major speaking event.

Sebastiano Cossu is a software engineer and game developer. He has worked on many AAA games on consoles, PCs, and mobile. He also contributed to the making of *Total War: Rome Remastered*. He is a lecturer at a prestigious Italian academy. He authored the Apress books *Game Development with GameMaker Studio 2* (2019) and *Beginning Game AI with Unity* (2021).

Acknowledgments

I would like to thank everyone who made this book possible.

A huge thank you to Apress, to the technical review and editorial teams, to the friends and family that have been so incredibly supportive, and to the incredible folks at Unity who made ML-Agents possible alongside the outstanding teams and communities involved in PyTorch.

And, last but not least, to my loving partner, for her incredible support and patience in dealing with the many late nights.

Thank you.

Introduction

Explore the world of machine learning through Unity ML-Agents. In this book, you'll learn about the impact of artificial intelligence and learn to build a reinforcement learning agent using the Unity ML-Agents package.

It's strongly recommended to go into this book with a solid understanding of the Unity engine and C#. The instructional chapters are written for Microsoft Windows 10, and some steps may vary across operating systems.

The book also includes a sample repository with the code we will cover in this book and the solution to the challenge proposed in Chapter 8.

You can access this repository at the following URL: `https://github.com/apress/introduction-unity-ml-agents`.

CHAPTER 1

Introduction

Artificial intelligence is the future, transforming the world around us, from self-driving vehicles to writing the first line in this book. Yet, like every other technology that came before it, there will be potential for good and evil. How this technology transforms society is up to us.

This technology will be the key to everything, from how we work and live to how we think.

We'll be exploring AI's deep and rich history, delving into what makes up a neural network, the ethical impacts, and broad concepts within the field of artificial intelligence – all before digging into the main topic, ML-Agents in Unity, where you'll learn to create your very own machine learning agents to solve complex problems with the potential for real-world impact.

What Is Machine Learning?

Machine learning, neural networks, deep learning, and artificial intelligence are all words that you've already heard. While these terms are similar, they do have differences.

Artificial intelligence is a field of computer science in which we give a machine the ability to algorithmically process data and make decisions. On the other hand, machine learning is a subset of artificial intelligence covering the process in which a machine learns to think, much like the human brain in a process called reinforcement learning.

D. Engelbrecht, *Introduction to Unity ML-Agents*,
https://doi.org/10.1007/978-1-4842-8998-3_1

The term "thinking" here is used loosely, as our current machine learning techniques have limitations – and are rather hyperoptimization algorithms that learn to optimize for a given outcome that yields the highest success criteria – often reward.

Machine learning enables software to improve its results over time without explicitly being programmed how to do so. Instead, we program the inputs and observations and let the AI figure out the best outcome.

Machine learning allows us to leverage machines to solve problems that are either too complex or time-consuming to program explicitly. Often, artificial intelligence will enable us to solve problems and challenges with greater accuracy than traditional software or even human ability.

So, where is machine learning used in the modern day? Let's dive into some of the most common use cases for machine learning in the modern era.

How We Use Machine Learning in the Modern Day

Where does machine learning get used? Machine learning has gained supremacy over traditional software in many domains. It may or may not surprise you to find how intertwined machine learning is with your everyday life and society as a whole.

Machine learning is also a rapidly growing market, with an estimated annual growth rate of 44%. Let's take a look at some of these use cases.

Serving Content Recommendations

Have you ever used products like YouTube Music or Spotify? Netflix? Or perhaps TikTok? These products can serve us customized content choices within minutes of using them, almost perfectly to our tastes.

These various platforms and products use machine learning to evaluate the content you might be interested in and prioritize content that would keep you engaged and using the product for longer. The platform serves content that you enjoy, thus driving engagement and, in turn, revenue – and it's all powered by machine learning.

ML, or machine learning, does this by taking various metrics, such as time watched, app usage, and exit points, to generate a reward/penalty score associated with the type of content. The platform uses the reward/penalty score to train an ML network to most accurately judge what kind of content will keep you, as a user, engaged for the longest.

Since you get content relevant to your tastes, you stay on the application for longer, view more adverts, or are more inclined to pay for a subscription, driving revenue growth for the company.

Autonomous Vehicles

A possible future is that most of our transport runs completely independent of human intervention. This future is the goal for autonomous vehicles, such as self-driving cars, an advanced autopilot for aircraft, and various public transport sectors.

Self-driving cars have become somewhat of exponential technological growth, with companies like Tesla at the forefront of this incredible technological innovation. ML empowers vehicles to make decisions rapidly and effectively where conventional software would struggle.

The approach to fully autonomous vehicles is still an ongoing field but typically includes multilayered ML approaches. A typical approach in autonomous vehicle AI is to use an ML agent to identify the environment around the vehicle and parse that information into a virtual reconstruction.

Another ML agent or traditional software-based solution can then use this reconstruction to make real-time decisions.

We can expand autonomous vehicle AI further by allowing autonomous vehicles to communicate with one another, sharing information and data for an additional layer of spatial awareness.

Power and Electrical Grid Management

Humanity is producing and consuming more power than ever, with electrical grids becoming far more complicated.

Traditional software systems are great as a foundation for these complex electrical networks but struggle to adapt to fluctuating power usage. We can use ML to optimize these electrical grids to predict network usage and load, thus saving electrical companies money and providing humanity with less wasted energy – and leaving a smaller carbon footprint.

Vaccines and Medical Drugs

ML has proven to be an incredible tool for fighting viruses by assisting scientists in creating various vaccines and effective medical drugs. Machine learning can conceive of protein structures in a process known as "folding" that would take conventional methods and software years to achieve.

Farming

AI enables farmers to achieve higher crop yields with improved quality in a process known as precision agriculture. We can achieve this precision agriculture by optimizing watering cycles to powering farming robotics that is becoming increasingly popular on various farms.

Security and Surveillance

Security is another domain that significantly benefits from advances in artificial intelligence and machine learning. From identifying suspected criminals to routing security personnel, ML has its part to play. ML is also a key technology in surveillance, a topic that we'll discuss later in this book, where we'll discuss the ethical implications.

Military

War never changes. Any technology that we can militarize will be. This point is especially true for a robust technology like machine learning. Various military powers leverage the power of ML to create powerful, intelligent weapons and defense systems and even assist with tactical planning and broad predictions.

Military applications of ML are also a domain that should be subject to moral and ethical debates, as weaponized artificial intelligence poses a severe risk to humanity if used carelessly.

City Planning

City planning is a sector where machine learning has incredible potential if used correctly concerning the privacy and freedom of its citizens. As our technology evolves, so do our cities. Various cities worldwide are incorporating machine learning to optimize how we plan our roads, route our traffic, monitor and police crime, and various other elements.

Prerequisites

To get the most out of this book, you'll occasionally need to get example code from the GitHub repository, which I will link throughout the book. This book does assume that you have experience in C# and a decent understanding of Unity3D.

Finally, you will also need some pretty significant hardware. I would suggest at least 32GB of RAM – 64GB of RAM if you intend to train more advanced models. Additionally, a good CPU is also a requirement.

Conclusion

In this chapter, we looked at what we'll cover in this book. We touched on the prerequisites you'll need to get the most out of this book, and we explored the various use cases for ML and AI today and how it's starting to shape our modern society.

We'll look at the configuration and setup of these prerequisites later in the book. In the next chapter, let's start our journey by examining AI's history.

CHAPTER 2

History of AI and Where We Are Today

In this chapter, we'll explore the history of artificial intelligence and how it evolved into what it is today. We'll begin our story in the United Kingdom shortly after the Second World War.

The People Who Shaped Artificial Intelligence

Throughout recent history, incredible computer scientists and mathematicians have been at the forefront of AI research – from building machines with vacuum tubes capable of behaving similarly to neural networks in modern AI to founding key research divisions at major universities.

One of the most notable people in AI is a person by the name of Alan Turing, a name that you've likely heard before.

© Dylan Engelbrecht 2023
D. Engelbrecht, *Introduction to Unity ML-Agents*,
https://doi.org/10.1007/978-1-4842-8998-3_2

Alan Mathison Turing

Alan Turing is considered by many to be the father of modern computer science.

He was among the people who made significant contributions to modern computing and was deeply fascinated with machines capable of thought.

He also made various contributions to the world of cryptoanalysis, cracking the Enigma code during the Second World War.

Alan also created what he called the "imitation game," which later became known as the Turing test. The Turing test is a test of a machine's ability to demonstrate intelligent behavior indistinguishable or equivalent to a human being.

Turing introduced the test in his 1950 paper titled "Computing Machinery and Intelligence."

While the Turing test was originally designed to test a machine's ability to demonstrate intelligent behavior, there has been a debate that the Turing test is more of a test of deception than intelligence. This debate has largely been sparked by Google's LaMDA, or Language Model for Dialog Applications.

Regardless, to date, no machine has successfully beaten the Turing test, but perhaps someday soon, this may change.

John McCarthy

Considered the founder of artificial intelligence by many, computer scientist John McCarthy coauthored the paper that coined the term artificial intelligence along with Claude Shannon, Marvin Minsky, and Nathaniel Rochester.

Marvin Lee Minsky

Minsky was a computer scientist who helped shape artificial intelligence as it is today. He was a cofounder of MIT's AI Laboratory and wrote several publications on AI and philosophy.

Guido van Rossum

Guido is a programmer and creator of the massively successful and influential programming language Python.

I've included him due to his indirect contributions to the field of AI due to the influential nature of the programming language he wrote.

Modern-Day Companies Paving the Future of AI

We've looked at a few people who helped shape the early history of artificial intelligence and paved the road for more advancements in the field.

However, modern-day AI advancements have become enormous feats of engineering involving sizeable teams and significant funding. As such, companies and their teams accomplish most AI developments in the modern day.

Let's look at some of the most noteworthy companies and their contributions to the field of artificial intelligence.

Python Software Foundation

While not focused on artificial intelligence, the Python Software Foundation has indirectly made significant contributions to the world of AI through fostering the development and community of the popular programming language Python.

Python has become one of the most popular languages for working with and developing artificial intelligence.

Python's success within the AI domain is likely due to the consistency and simplicity of its design. Python has amassed an incredible library of codebases for manipulating and interpreting data and powerful machine learning frameworks, most notably PyTorch and TensorFlow. We'll discuss these frameworks later in the book.

Still, without the Python Software Foundation, Guido van Rossum, and the massive community collaboration, AI and machine learning would be far behind where it is today.

Nvidia

Nvidia is a company with a diverse range of products, from graphics cards to data center CPU chips all the way to consumer-level gaming hardware. Nvidia is a massive contender within the world of artificial intelligence research, especially for its work on CUDA or Compute Unified Device Architecture. CUDA has been a significant advantage for machine learning, as it allows the software to perform general-purpose processing on GPUs that support the architecture, significantly improving AI performance.

They leverage artificial intelligence and machine learning to power self-driving cars, provide better graphics performance for consumer gaming, and power intelligent machines.

The company even uses artificial intelligence to improve its chip design, a considerable step toward machines capable of self-improvement.

Jensen Huang founded Nvidia in April 1993, primarily focusing on PC graphics, where it helped the gaming industry become the massively successful market it is today.

Talking about hardware, the next company is IBM.

IBM

International Business Machines, or IBM, is a company rooted in the origins of modern computing. IBM created some of the first supercomputers used for artificial intelligence.

One such supercomputer is Deep Blue, an iconic machine that was the first to beat the former reigning chess world champion, Garry Kasparov. This victory resulted in Deep Blue being the first machine capable of winning against a world champion chess player and marked a significant milestone in the development of artificial intelligence.

IBM has since contributed to the development of artificial intelligence and developed Watson, an AI named after the founder and first CEO of IBM, Thomas J. Watson. Watson is capable of answering questions asked in natural language and was able to beat human players in the game *Jeopardy!*.

Google

Google is a household name and far more than just a search engine. Google has contributed to the world of AI and machine learning through self-driving cars, cloud computing, and AI research and development.

This company is responsible for the development of several AI technologies, namely:

- **AutoML** – AutoML is a product developed by Google that attempts to democratize AI by allowing developers with limited exposure to machine learning to build and train quality artificial intelligence models to suit their business needs.

- **Transformer** – Transformer is a novel AI architecture intended for conversational AI development.

- **LaMDA AI** – LaMDA is a conversational artificial intelligence capable of remarkable conversational skills. Google built LaMDA atop its Transformer architecture.

Tesla

Electric vehicle (EV) company Tesla has made significant advancements in AI with their self-driving car technology.

Tesla uses a hybrid approach to self-driving vehicles, using AI to interpret the data from the vehicles' various sensors to reconstruct a virtual environment where the car can follow programmed rules to drive. These commands are then sent to the vehicle, causing it to operate, seldom needing a driver's input.

Tesla plans to use this virtual reconstruction AI in possible future Tesla products, such as their AI helper robot, Optimus – a general-purpose robotic humanoid.

Tesla's founders include Elon Musk, a business magnet who also founded various other companies that utilize AI in some form or another; among them include

- **SpaceX** – Registered as Space Exploration Technologies Corp. SpaceX is a space launch provider, spacecraft manufacturer, and, more recently, a satellite communications company. SpaceX uses an AI-powered autopilot that allows its rockets to navigate from the launch pad and dock with the International Space Station.

- **Neuralink** – Neuralink is another company founded by Elon Musk. Neuralink aims to create a powerful brain-to-computer interface technology called Neuralink and uses advanced AI to interpret and parse signals received from the thousands of Neuralink sensors in the brain.

- **OpenAI** – OpenAI is the more relevant company on this list for the book. Elon Musk is one of the founders of OpenAI, a research lab that started as a nonprofit but later split into two entities, the for-profit OpenAI LP and the nonprofit OpenAI Inc.

OpenAI has contributed to AI and ML and made significant landmark achievements, such as creating an AI that beat the *Dota 2* world champions. It also created AI models such as DALL-E, capable of creating realistic images from a piece of text, and GPT-3, a powerful model capable of writing code, among other things.

Let's look further at OpenAI, the next company on the list.

OpenAI

OpenAI aims to further the field of AI, aiming for the long-term goal of creating a safe AGI – or artificial general intelligence.

An AGI is an AI that can perform several different tasks and overcome various challenges rather than being trained in a single task. OpenAI has created a variety of AI and ML agents throughout its existence, from GPT to DALL-E.

They also made OpenAI Five, a team of five AI agents that defeated the reigning *Dota 2* championship team, OG – 2:0. This incredible engineering feat demonstrated AI's ability to achieve expert-level performance, learn human-AI cooperation, and operate at an Internet scale.

How AI Has Evolved in Games, from Chess to *Dota 2*

AI has a long history in games – from games as old as chess to modern video games like the successful *Dota 2*. Researchers once believed that the pinnacle of artificial intelligence would be the day that AI could beat a grandmaster at chess.

There was a belief that AI would need to be conscious to think well enough to play chess. This belief turned out to be far from the truth; while Deep Blue's chess victory was a crowning achievement in the world of AI, it was only the first mile of the road that we're on today.

With the impressive funding and rise of massive development studios focusing on machine learning and AI, we've seen technologies and AI advancements surpass the earlier Deep Blue. In more recent history, OpenAI created their OpenAI Five. This AI agent can interpret pixel data from the screen and make decisions in a complex *Dota 2* game alone and in AAM.

AI in games isn't always machine learning. Most game AI is hardcoded logic, often purposefully made to make mistakes. An AI that's better than the best human players is not fun for the average human player. Hybrid approaches to hardcoded AI and machine learning for game AI are a trend in the game development industry.

So, Where Are We Now with AI in Game Development?

Much of the work and research on machine learning in the game development industry focuses on reducing labor-intensive and monotonous tasks. AI is a powerhouse when it comes to game tools.

Let's look at a few examples of how AI technologies can aid us in building powerful tools that free up artists, programmers, and designers so that we can focus on innovating rather than monotonous boilerplate work.

GitHub Copilot

If you're a developer, you're well familiar with GitHub, and if you've kept your finger on the pulse of industry-changing technologies, then you may have heard of GitHub copilot.

Copilot is an AI pair programmer. The concept of pair programming has been around for a long time, where you and another developer sit and watch the same screen while programming. Pair programming allows you to share ideas rapidly, brainstorm code solutions, check for errors, and improve the overall quality of the code.

The problem is you don't always have another developer to pair-program with – so what if we could have a neural network fill that role for you? Impossible? It turns out programming languages are similar to spoken languages – so much so that GitHub was able to take OpenAI's GPT-3 agent and train it on the entirety of its open source codebase.

Out of this comes GitHub copilot, an AI agent capable of suggesting code, writing entire boilerplate classes, and even writing and completing code comments. While it does require a knowledgeable developer to review the suggestions, it does a pretty good job of automating many less exciting tasks.

While copilot is incredibly powerful, it has sparked an ethical dilemma – if an AI writes code, who owns that code? This copyright gray area rings true, especially if a company trains an AI on another company or developers' code. That said, GitHub copilot only uses open source code as training data for the agent, so one may be able to compare it to a developer learning from another developer since the AI doesn't directly copy the code.

We'll discuss many more ethical dilemmas AI brings to the table later in this book.

Let's move on to the next AI agent powering game development tools – one capable of generating novel animations from training data.

A Neural State Machine for Character-Scene Interactions

One such example is a neural state machine proposed by authors Sebastian Starke, He Zhang, Taku Komura, and Jun Saito in their research paper titled "Neural state machine for character-scene interactions." You can read their research at https://doi.org/10.1145/3355089.3356505.

A neural state machine is a form of character animation controller. The neural state machine is a neural network that dynamically creates novel animations for a game character based on the context of the situation, user input, and creative input from the art team. The agent then uses reference and training data to create novel, fluid, and near-perfect animations.

The impressive part is the ability of the neural network to take information about the character's immediate environment to better tailor the animations to the situation.

The agent voxelized the geometry in the surrounding environment and parses that data to make decisions in real time about its environment.

Another tool we're going to look at is a language model, rather than a tool, but it may aid researchers and developers in creating tools accessible to the average developer, artist, or designer. Let's take a look at BLOOM, a large language model that's accessible and open source.

BLOOM, a BigScience Initiative

Most large language models have been inaccessible to developers, with strict restrictions on commercial use. This closed nature of large models is understandable due to the expensive nature of training models. The second factor is that large AI companies use these models in their products, so giving everyone access would not make business sense. Thirdly, powerful open source AI models pose ethical risks and concerns.

This caveat of access is where BLOOM comes in. BLOOM is the largest open source LLM, or large language model, recently released.

BLOOM features an astounding 176 billion parameters compared to GPT-3's full model, which contains 173 billion. BLOOM has more parameters and supports many more languages, and due to its open source nature, it supports 56 languages.

All of this, and BLOOM is entirely open source, with a "RAIL" license, short for Responsible AI License. Developers and researchers trained BLOOM on France's Jean Zay supercomputer, thanks to a compute grant worth an estimated €3M from research agencies, CNRS and GENCI.

You can access BLOOM at the following link: `https://huggingface.co/bigscience/bloom`.

Conclusion

In this chapter, we dove into the history of AI. We explored and learned about the various people and companies that made AI what it is today. In the following chapter, we'll look into the future of AI and where this technology could take our society.

We'll also explore the ethical ramifications of this technology and discuss how we can mitigate the risks of AI development.

CHAPTER 3

The Future of AI and Ethical Implications

In the previous chapter, we discussed the origins of AI and the people and companies that shaped where we are today. In this chapter, we'll glance at what the future of AI might hold and how it could impact our society and discuss the ethical implications of AI and why we need to develop AI responsibly with these factors in mind.

AI has a long road ahead, with us developers at its forefront. It's up to us to build AI in a way that contributes positively to humanity.

To do so, we need to consider the future of AI development and how it may affect the lives of people who use it – directly or indirectly. It's up to us as developers to ensure that our AI benefits humanity.

To achieve this, we need to develop inclusive AI, mitigate bias in our training data, and expand on AI research. Let's look into what the future of AI might hold in the coming decades.

© Dylan Engelbrecht 2023
D. Engelbrecht, *Introduction to Unity ML-Agents*,
https://doi.org/10.1007/978-1-4842-8998-3_3

The Future of AI

To better understand how to develop responsible AI, we need to picture what the future might look like with responsible AI.

Law and Justice

AI has the potential to revolutionize the judiciary system. A possible future might offer AI agents capable of providing everyone with access to affordable legal protection and a fair means of prosecution and judgment, free of bias.

Law is at the heart of our society. Businesses, daily life, and rights are all affected by it.

The legal services industry is massive – estimations exceeded $700 billion in 2020. Yet, legal services are often out of reach to lower-class households; the ones who need it most cannot afford good legal services.

In the future, AI may prove vital in democratizing access to affordable legal services.

We could see AI lawyers, prosecutors, judges dealing with small claims, and lower-end legal services. Having AI involved in law could provide unbiased rulings or assist human lawyers with higher-end cases.

The risk here, however, is that for AI to provide unbiased legal services, we will need to eliminate bias in training data – one of AI's biggest challenges.

AI could help lawyers find the best course of action for a legal case in a world where we have nearly eliminated bias from training data.

This assistance could be anywhere from removing the monotonous work of combing through past cases to providing the public with automated legal services at a highly affordable rate.

Healthcare

Another great field that AI can contribute to is healthcare. We could train AI agents to assist doctors in diagnosing patients, minimize human error in surgery, and pave the way for further advancements in vaccine research.

This AI assistance could dramatically reduce the cost of surgeries and make healthcare more affordable and available to everyone. AI-powered robotics could even perform specialist surgeries, giving low-income households lifesaving access to brain surgeries and other specialist operations.

One might think AI-powered robotics would not be able to perform on par with human surgeries, but robots are far more accurate than the human hand. It's why surgeons use robots like the da Vinci Surgical System.

Neuralink and Card79 are already developing other excellent examples of surgery robotics.

Neuralink is developing a robot with its industrial design partner, Card79, capable of performing the brain surgery required for the Neuralink brain-to-computer interface chip.

The long-term goal of Neuralink is to keep humanity relevant with the next generations of AI.

But that's just one area of healthcare.

AI is also exceptional at folding protein structures, where the final structures of proteins are calculated, a slow and costly process in traditional environments. However, with the use of AI, the cost of protein folding has gone down dramatically.

Recently, Google made a significant contribution to this field with its AlphaFold AI.

This technology will enable researchers to synthesize various new drugs and medications, hopefully someday curing human disease or, at the very least, making all diseases and conditions treatable within the coming decades.

In the coming decades, we may see a day when medication is affordable and easily accessible to those who need it – genuinely giving everyone the right to affordable healthcare, regardless of socioeconomic standing.

Taxes and Governance

In the coming decades, we may see the adoption of ML agents for designing, or at least assisting with, the development of fair taxation policies that do not impede innovation.

Research into the feasibility of ML development of taxation policies is already well underway, with promising results.

A great example of this research is a paper by Stephan Zheng, Alexander Trott, Sunil Srinivasa, David C. Parkes, and Richard Socher, titled "The AI Economist: Taxation policy design via two-level deep multiagent reinforcement learning."

You can read the full paper with the following DOI:10.1126/sciadv.abk2607

The paper proposes using multiagent ML agents to optimize taxation policies using reinforcement learning. This optimization focuses on balancing equality and productivity.

The research uses ML agents in a simulated environment to simulate an economy consisting of both a single-step economy and a gather-trade-build economy. The AI agents representing economy participants and the AI that manages policies learn to adapt to each other.

The paper's results indicate that an AI policy maker provides various advantages over traditional systems and could be helpful in policy making in the future.

So, it's not far off to imagine a world in which taxation policies are primarily driven by AI agents continually adapting to the economic climate and the world around us. A policy AI in the future could redistribute wealth where it's needed, invest in infrastructure, and adapt as needed – with far better foresight than human policy makers.

This sense of fairness could increase taxpayer confidence and allow even more efficient taxation.

Next, let's examine how AI may even help us with life extension and how AI might revolutionize how we interact with the machines and devices around us or even each other.

Life Extension and Brain-Computer Interfaces

Extending human life has been a goal for humanity for centuries, from folklore to modern medicine. We're finally reaching a point in our society where we're starting to understand the building blocks of the human body.

Various companies are working on prolonging human life, enabling us to lead longer, healthier lives. Machine learning enables these companies to synthesize new drugs and better understand our cells.

On the other side, we have brain-computer interfaces or BCIs for short.

The BCI side of technology has been relatively slow to advance, likely due to the most invasive technology, high cost, and low consumer use cases outside those who use BCIs as a disability aid.

But what if we used BCI for more than aiding disabilities? The technology can potentially treat disability, brain disease, and possibly, one day, even death. And according to Elon Musk, it might even save us from AI.

If artificial superintelligence emerged, it could likely make humans obsolete as an AI of this nature could far exceed any human intelligence.

In such a case, we would need a way to remain relevant. Neural technology company, Neuralink, was founded for that exact reason as its long-term goal. In the coming decades, Neuralink aims to create a consumer-grade BCI capable of two-way communication between a user's brain and electronic devices.

This advanced BCI would, in theory, create a form of AI layer for our brains, allowing us to utilize technology to boost our mental capacity. The

BCI could use AI to interpret our brain signals, allowing the machine to understand the user's thoughts.

However, it doesn't stop there. According to Ray Kurzweil, an American inventor and futurist, we may see digital mind uploading perfected by the mid-2030s.

Digital mind uploading is the concept of fully reconstructing the human brain within a simulated space, allowing humans to become entirely software based if they choose to.

Ray Kurzweil specializes in AI research at Google and has made many accurate estimations on the progress of technology over the years.

So perhaps it's not so far-fetched to believe that humans might become software based in the coming decades in the evolutionary race against the AI we create.

Entertainment

AI is becoming more intertwined with our entertainment and how companies serve us content and AI-generated content, which we may see become more prevalent in our society over the coming years and decades.

We may see AI-generated art and music become more prevalent – and AI assistants helping writers build their worlds. AI-generated art is already becoming easily accessible to the average user. AI is also capable of creating music that – at least in my opinion – is pretty good.

One such AI is Nvidia's AIVA, Artificial Intelligence Virtual Artist, capable of producing incredibly detailed and sophisticated musical pieces.

Another AI tool comes from the company Amper Music. Musician Taryn Southern created an incredible song using AI tools. It showcases what's achievable today. The song is called "Break Free" by Taryn Southern.

For creating the song, Taryn used a combination of various AI tools – with lyrics and vocals done by her. She created the visuals with Deep

Dream Generator, vocal production and arrangement by Ethan Carlson, and the music is composed by Amper AI.

These songs show how powerful AI is today, but in the coming decades, we're likely to see AI composers become more prevalent in everyday entertainment. From music to game music, AI will be almost everywhere in some form or another.

AI and human artists can fill in for each other's weaknesses, enabling artists to create incredible work.

Avoiding a Bad Future

We've looked at what the future of AI might hold for various industries and aspects of our society. However, if we as AI researchers and developers are irresponsible with our AI research, the future could look a whole lot different in all the wrong ways.

We need to be conscious of the ripple effects that AI will have as it becomes exponentially more adept at its tasks and ensure that we extend a hand to those who can't keep up in industries where AI may negatively affect job availability.

A bad future could see the divide between rich and poor reach extreme levels, or at the extreme, it could mean the extinction of humanity.

As those leading the field, we must ensure that we develop AI with ethics in mind.

To do that, we should understand that AI has the possibility of replacing jobs and the livelihoods of people around the world and instead should either ensure that it creates better jobs for humans or augments the lives of those that use it instead of replacing them.

Let's avoid a bad future and develop diverse and inclusive AI for the betterment of humankind.

How do we do that? It starts with understanding bias and how bias negatively affects AI and humanity.

Bias and Why We Need Diverse Datasets

Next, we'll discuss why bias is bad for AI and why it could negatively impact society, but to do that, we first need to understand what bias is in AI terms.

So, What Is Bias in AI?

Much like society has stereotypes and biases, bias in AI refers to an AI's inclination or prejudice toward the information we give it. This bias often manifests as stereotypes or other exclusionary forms that don't consider the diverse society that makes up the world.

This bias can take form in many different ways, from AI not recognizing the voice of a minority group in a speech-to-text application to facial recognition tagging a minority group as an animal rather than a person.

This bias breaks down much of society's progress over the past few years in self-correcting and reducing stereotypes and prejudices and can dehumanize people worldwide.

We're all in this together, and it's up to us to create an AI that respects cultures, beliefs, and people. Regardless of race, gender, nationality, language, or other categories, terrible people have used to divide humanity in the past.

So how do we reduce bias?

Why We Need Diverse Datasets

It all comes down to how we train our AI. AI requires massive amounts of data to learn from, but often that data that we train it on is based on our imperfect society. Because of that, it's common for people to use datasets skewed toward a particular demographic or culture.

Worst of all, it's often very challenging to identify bias in datasets due to how large they are. Without researchers focusing on inclusion in AI, we risk reinforcing old, bad habits in our society.

But how do we fix it?

A proposed solution is to use diverse datasets. Diverse datasets contain datasets from varying locations, with different cultures and minorities equally distributed with other groups.

Diversifying datasets allows AI to see the world from different perspectives, reducing bias. The technique is not perfect, but it's a start – and perhaps someday, we will have AI capable of self-correcting bias.

Discussing the Moral and Ethical Implications

We've discussed some of the ways that AI might impact our society in the coming decades and some of the challenges it already faces today concerning bias and prejudice.

Apart from the risk of bias and a potential threat of job loss, there are some questions that we need to start asking now. One of the many conversations we need is, what happens when an AI proves to be sentient or self-aware?

If an artificial general intelligence (AGI) claims to be self-aware, what consequences would that have on society when we're the only self-aware and intelligent civilization we know about, and how do we prove if an AI is self-aware or simply faking it?

With narrow AIs already becoming good enough to fool engineers into believing that they are self-aware, as in the recent case of a Google engineer being put on leave, how does one begin to prove or disprove self-awareness in the case of an AGI with a presumably more extensive and more complex neural network?

So we must now ask these questions, inspire younger generations to do the same, and encourage AI researchers and developers to create AI responsibly.

Why AI?

If AI is a double-edged sword, then why should we craft them? AI has the potential to be humanity's most incredible creation, something capable of solving problems that traditional software cannot.

Traditional software also requires extensive labor to maintain and update. Coupled with a growing global codebase, we will see a lack of skilled and experienced software engineers become even more prevalent than today.

On the other hand, AI software could ease software engineering workload by adapting to new information without human intervention.

Flavors of AI

AI is quite a broad term, and it's about time we start breaking it down and learning more about different classifications of AI and various approaches to AI development.

In this chapter, we'll do just that. We will take a journey into what makes up artificial intelligence and how we broadly classify AI and explore various AI techniques.

We'll detail these different AI techniques and weigh the pros and cons. We'll then focus on machine learning and discuss the methods that power Unity's ML-Agents.

Finally, we'll wrap up this chapter by discussing some practical use cases for Unity ML-Agents.

AI Road Map and Classification

As I've mentioned earlier, artificial intelligence is a broad term encompassing various techniques used to simulate human intelligence, but not all AI is as advanced as you might think.

I'd go so far as to say that AI is still in its infancy today, and we've only begun to scratch the surface. As we've started moving through the road map, AI's exponential growth has influenced our society, changed how we live, and much more.

Let's look at the road map of different AI classifications and see where we are today (Figure 3-1).

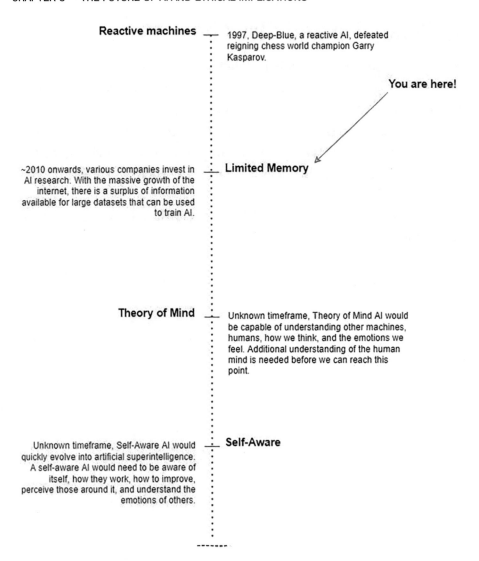

Reactive machines — 1997, Deep-Blue, a reactive AI, defeated reigning chess world champion Garry Kasparov.

You are here!

~2010 onwards, various companies invest in AI research. With the massive growth of the internet, there is a surplus of information available for large datasets that can be used to train AI. — **Limited Memory**

Theory of Mind — Unknown timeframe, Theory of Mind AI would be capable of understanding other machines, humans, how we think, and the emotions we feel. Additional understanding of the human mind is needed before we can reach this point.

Unknown timeframe, Self-Aware AI would quickly evolve into artificial superintelligence. A self-aware AI would need to be aware of itself, how they work, how to improve, perceive those around it, and understand the emotions of others. — **Self-Aware**

Figure 3-1. *The timeline depicts where we are with AI development*

Reactive Machines

The most basic of AI – and one of the earliest – are called reactive machines. These AI systems retain no memory of previous events and purely react to the current information they receive.

A great example of reactive AI is that of Deep Blue, the AI system developed by IBM that we discussed in a previous chapter.

Deep Blue could only take a current set of parameters and determine the next chess move.

This extremely narrow focus leads to an issue where Deep Blue would encounter situations where it would repeat actions, leading to a stalemate in chess.

So, to help Deep Blue, its developers gave it a single rule – not to repeat any move more than three times.

A reactive machine cannot solve problems outside of the specific tasks given due to an inability to recall prior information.

This flaw makes them much like traditional computer software.

The key distinguishing factor that makes an AI system purely reactive is that if given the same parameters, it will respond identically to the situation every time.

We've come a long way since reactive machines – and they still have their place – but we're still pretty early on in the road map.

The key takeaways here are as follows:

- Reactive machines are the most basic form of AI.

- IBM's Deep Blue is an example of a reactive AI.

- Reactive machines cannot recall prior information.

- Given the same parameters, it will respond identically to the same situation every time.

The next type of AI we'll discuss is limited memory AI.

Limited Memory

We're here!

Limited memory AI systems are what we're currently working on. It has provided an incredible upgrade from traditional reactive networks.

The AI agents of today can sift through years and years of data for training and can recall prior experiences to improve.

This ability to leverage memory to continue learning enables us to build self-driving cars capable of becoming better and better at driving.

It enables us to build AI agents capable of beating championship teams in complex 3D games.

Limited memory AI is still quite a broad topic, and we'll continue to break it down further in this chapter when we discuss modern AI techniques.

These AI systems are goal oriented rather than solving a single task like their predecessor.

One could subclassify a limited memory AI as a narrow artificial intelligence.

They typically require large datasets surrounding the specific goal it needs to achieve.

So, the most important things to note about limited memory AI are as follows:

- Our current technology is at the point of limited memory AI.

- Limited memory AI can utilize years of data for training.

- These AI systems can recall prior experiences for improvement.

- Limited memory AI is goal oriented.

While limited memory machines are impressive, it's unable to truly understand what it is doing or the data it is using.

That brings us to the following classification on the road map.

While limited memory machines cannot understand the world around them, we expect a theory of mind AI systems to excel by leveraging understanding.

So what is a theory of mind AI system?

Theory of Mind

These AI systems will be far more complex than any before.

These AI systems will be able to understand the world around them, the emotions of the people surrounding them, and more.

The big difference between a theory of mind AI and limited memory AI is that instead of just completing a task based on training data, they will understand the tasks they perform.

These AI systems will be able to interpret and understand our emotions – possibly even showing signs of empathy. Theory of mind AI will likely become the first artificial general intelligence or AGI.

Once an AI system understands its actions, we will need to answer the moral and ethical questions we asked in a previous chapter.

As you can see, this might be a lot sooner than expected, so we need to start asking these questions today.

While some classify AGI as entirely separate from the theory of mind AI systems, we might see these lines blurred.

Based on current AI progress, I anticipate the first AGI to come within ten years of the theory of mind AI systems because of how intertwined they are.

The critical things to remember here are as follows:

- Theory of mind AI is a hypothetical AI system.

- They would be capable of understanding.

- They could have the ability to understand emotion.

- They could perhaps show empathy.

- Theory of mind AI would quickly lead to AGI.

Let's take a look at AGI.

Artificial General Intelligence (AGI)

AGI is a theory of mind AI system capable of performing a generalized set of tasks – instead of only being able to perform a single task.

This AI will be far superior to prior AI systems, but we're still unsure how to achieve a theory of mind AI or AGI.

Researchers have made various attempts to string together multiple limited memory AI agents.

However, it's unclear if this will lead to AGI, as it still does not allow the AI to understand the tasks that it performs.

One might view that approach as comparing a Swiss Army knife to an engineer.

The benefit of AGI is that we may be able to utilize them to assist with the creation of the next generation of artificial intelligence, self-aware AI.

Self-aware AI will be able to understand itself, as well as be able to outperform any traditional AI system. Let's take a deeper look at what self-aware AI might look like in the future.

Self-Aware

A self-aware AI system is capable of understanding not only the tasks that they perform, but they are also capable of understanding the inner working of the self.

This ability to introspect will likely result in massive and rapid self-improvement, quickly reaching a point that could make any nonaugmented human intelligence obsolete.

The massive development spike of AI will likely result in the first artificial superintelligence.

Much like AGI, some classify artificial superintelligence as a separate category.

But due to how fast a self-aware AI agent would be able to improve, I anticipate that we'll see the first ASI within one to three years of a self-aware AI tasked with self-improvement. Due to that, I include it within the self-aware category.

Finally, the important takeaways here are as follows:

- Self-aware AI is hypothetical and does not exist yet.

- A self-aware AI system would be capable of introspection.

- Self-aware AI would understand the tasks that they are performing.

- They will likely result in a massive development spike of AI.

- Self-aware AI will likely rapidly evolve into artificial superintelligence.

Let's look at what an ASI might be capable of in the future.

Artificial Superintelligence (ASI)

AI researchers classify artificial superintelligence as an AI agent capable of intelligence far exceeding that of the brightest and most gifted human minds.

The challenge lies in creating artificial superintelligence that benefits humanity. As philosopher and AI researcher Nick Bostrom said, "We only have one chance at this."

Bostrom proposed a potential solution for artificial superintelligence, in which we use AI to learn what humanity values. The artificial superintelligence could then use these learned values to drive its goals.

So going further into this book, you might become a part of the team that creates the first artificial superintelligence. I implore you to consider all aspects to create a safe ASI that works in unison with humanity for a better future.

Let's jump back to the modern day, discussing various techniques and types of limited memory AI and how Unity ML-Agents use these techniques.

Machine Learning with Unity ML-Agents

We use the Unity Machine Learning Agents package to create machine learning systems in Unity.

The Unity ML-Agents package is a wrapper allowing Unity to interface with a popular AI framework called PyTorch.

By connecting Unity and PyTorch, we can create virtual training environments for our agents, enabling powerful game or simulation AI.

We typically train ML-Agents using either a single or combination of the following techniques:

- Reinforcement learning

- Imitation learning

- Neuroevolution

However, it's not limited to these techniques. You can also leverage the easy-to-use API to use almost any AI technique you build in Python.

Let's look at these techniques in more detail.

Reinforcement Learning

One of the most common techniques we use with ML-Agents, often in tandem with other techniques, is reinforcement learning.

Reinforcement learning allows us to dictate goals by carefully tweaking rewards based on the ML-Agent's actions.

Much like training an animal, when the animal performs the desired action, we provide a reward to the agent.

Inversely, if the agent fails at the task or performs negatively, we give a punishment – essentially a negative reward.

In the context of AI, we typically measure a reward as a value.

As the agent trains, it learns what actions based on what inputs result in positive or negative rewards and attempts to achieve the highest reward value possible.

We'll be discussing rewards in more detail in the next chapter.

With reinforcement learning, we typically have an agent with access to various inputs and outputs.

We then allow it to make decisions based on the input and training data. Once the agent decides, it performs an action consisting of various output values.

Based on the result of that action, we then reward or punish the agent.

We then repeat this flow until the desired level of training is reached or a researcher stops the training to make adjustments.

As the training cycles continue, the agent improves its abilities in a step commonly referred to as a policy change step to complete the given task.

This method of AI training is potent but has its downfalls, often remedied by using this technique in combination with another method.

Reinforcement agent flows typically look something like Figure 3-2.

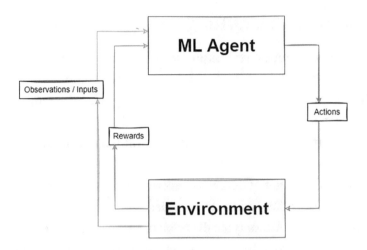

Figure 3-2. *The typical training cycle of a reinforcement learning agent*

We'll discuss the various algorithms used in reinforcement learning later in the book as we get deeper into understanding Unity ML-Agents.

The major drawback of using reinforcement learning alone is training complex tasks becomes challenging.

It becomes complicated because, in reinforcement learning, the AI typically starts by giving almost random outputs to test what grants a reward and a punishment.

This approach is fine for simple tasks, but some tasks may only give rewards after the agent has performed multiple complex actions – actions that the AI may never try depending on the complexity and length of the task.

Thankfully, we can provide a helping hand by using reinforcement learning in tandem with imitation learning.

Let's look at imitation learning and see how we can use it to better train our agents.

Imitation Learning

Let's say we have a complex task for our new agent. The AI needs to push a block into place. Once the block is in place, it must walk around and over the block to reach the goal.

If we just use reinforcement learning, we would encounter some problems in this scenario, as the agent may find it challenging to understand the task.

If we reward the agent for reaching the goal, it may never figure out that it needs to push the block first. And on the other hand, if we assign a reward for moving the block into place, the agent may decide that moving the block in and out of place is an entirely valid answer, as it would receive a reward.

Both scenarios are impractical for training the agent for this task.

That's where imitation learning comes in.

Unity ML-Agents support imitation learning. Imitation learning allows us to show the AI how to complete the task, giving it a head start.

Imitation learning results in the agent quickly understanding the goal and reward mechanisms for the challenge.

Unity ML-Agents also allows us to use a variety of imitation learning algorithms to determine the policy change step, how curious the agent should be, and how much it should rely on following the imitation recording.

We'll discuss these algorithms later in the book.

Imitation learning on its own is not super practical, as the agent will never become better than the human that taught it. However, coupled with reinforcement learning, imitation learning quickly becomes a superior learning technique.

The combination of imitation and reinforcement learning allows an agent to pick up on the goals of the challenge quickly and, in many cases, become far superior to any human at the challenge.

Another technique that we have at our disposal is neuroevolution.

Neuroevolution

Neuroevolution is another technique, yet the concept dates back to before reinforcement learning or imitation learning. The idea behind neuroevolution is to allow a neural network to form and mutate, repeating throughout several computational generations.

You can specify the goal parameter using neuroevolution, and after each training step, only the best of the previous agents survive.

This evolutionary training approach makes neuroevolution much like biological evolution, where survival of the fittest is the rule.

However, nowadays, neuroevolution is typically used alongside other techniques.

Instead of building the neural network itself, we can use it to optimize hyperparameters. We'll discuss hyperparameters later in the book, but for some context, they are variables that we can tweak as developers and researchers.

Tweaking these hyperparameters allows us to alter training times, how effective a neural network can train, how curious a neural network is, and many other settings.

Practical Use Cases for Unity ML-Agents

Unity ML agents have many practical, real-world use case scenarios. Next, we'll look at some of these and how you may use ML agents to build something useful.

First and foremost, Unity has done a fantastic job of creating tools that are easy to understand and have opened machine learning up to whole new groups of people. One of the most notable use cases is that Unity ML-Agents is a great way to learn how to build machine learning agents!

Learning How to Build Machine Learning Agents

While it does require some understanding of the Unity game engine and some basic programming skills, ML-Agents is incredibly beginner friendly.

Because of the relatively low barrier to entry with ML-Agents, if you have a good understanding of Unity and C#, it makes for a fantastic way to branch into machine learning.

Unity has built several components that will help you get started quickly and easily – we'll discuss some of these later in the book and how to build your own.

With that said, having a solid experience of the engine and knowing your way around C# is what will open up the world of ML-Agents to you.

Self-Driving Cars

Due to the virtualized environment nature of Unity, ML-Agents are excellent at understanding virtual reconstructions of environments.

One could use Unity ML-Agents to power the self-driving cars of the future!

A great approach would be to have the ML-Agent be responsible for parsing the real world into a virtual construct and have another AI control the vehicle, or a conventional rule-based system makes the driving decisions.

With time, you could refine and perfect this approach, and one could even have multiple AI cars cross-communicating, allowing for redundancies or better world interpretation.

Game AI

ML-Agents can be used in many different ways within game development. First would be having AI agents within the game world controlled via an ML-Agent.

Second, one could use ML-Agents as a test framework for certain types of games with complex interactions where traditional automated testing solutions would struggle.

Let's talk about the former first.

ML-Agents could be a great way to power AI in games, and that's not to say it would be a great fit in every game. Just because you can make a system powered by ML doesn't necessarily mean it's the best approach. However, it does have a place.

ML-Agents is exceptionally good at casual games and can be used to power things like hints for hypercasual match-three-type games.

Or depending on how much time investment you would like to put into development, it can navigate 3D worlds or solve more complex puzzles.

While you may think the time investment is not worth it, you can leverage that trained model for the latter topic, ML-Agent-powered test frameworks. The idea here is that you take that trained model and use it as a form of automation testing, significantly reducing the workload of your quality assurance team.

Using ML-Agents in game development should be evaluated on a case-by-case basis, but we should not overlook the potential to use ML-Agents in game development.

Robotics

ML-Agents pair excellently with robotics. While this does require additional work of building an API for Unity to interact with your robotics, once done, you can create an ML-Agent that learns to use the robotics that you've made.

An AI claw robot that learns to pick up objects is an excellent example, but you're not limited to that.

Robotics pair well with Unity ML-Agents because robotics and electrical devices are typically controlled by normalized (when you put a value in between a range of zero and one) electrical values and receive normalized electrical signals from your sensors.

Since ML-Agents train best with normalized values, you don't need to work hard to ensure that your signals fall within the expected normalized ranges because they already do.

The significant challenge with robotics is creating an accurate digital twin simulation that you can use for training. This topic brings us to the next great use case, simulated spaces for agent training.

Simulated Space for Agent Training

The issue with training an AI on raw data signals from an external, real-world electrical device is that the ML-Agent needs to train for an extended period, from days to years.

We typically reduce this training time by parallelizing the learning work.

We do this by duplicating ML-Agent training environments, sometimes having many hundred ML-Agents train simultaneously.

This amount of ML-Agents all interfacing with real-world robotics would each require a robotic unit.

As you can quickly foresee, this would drive up costs and, in most situations, may be completely impractical due to the physical connectors required.

Another step we can take to speed up the training time is to speed up the simulation time.

As you can well imagine, mechanical components can only move so fast, so it becomes impractical to attempt to speed them up ten times their intended speed.

So instead, we create a digital twin representing the hardware that the ML-Agent will control.

A digital twin is an entirely virtual model designed to accurately reflect the physical object you're studying.

We can then use the digital twin of the robotic hardware in a simulated space to train several hundred ML-Agents simultaneously at ten times the intended speed.

Once we have trained the ML-Agent model to our satisfaction, we simply switch to using the robotic input and output signals.

We could then monitor the ML-Agent's control over the hardware to see if it meets our expected results.

Training Gym for Agents

We can take our training one step further. Unity ML-Agents has native support for OpenAI gym, an open source toolkit for developing and comparing reinforcement learning techniques.

Gym allows us to compare our techniques to optimize our ML-Agents. Gym is outside the scope of this book, though. However, if you're interested in digging deeper, you can read more about it in the following link: `https://github.com/openai/gym`.

Conclusion

That's it for this chapter. Next, we'll discuss in more detail how reinforcement learning uses rewards to train agents. Reward systems in AI are an exciting topic, but before we move on, let's recap what we covered in this chapter.

In this chapter, we explored the future of AI and envisioned how different AI technologies might impact our society, from using AI to interpret our brain signals to creating art.

We discussed how we need to consider diversity and aim to reduce bias in our datasets to prevent the mistakes of our society's past.

Then we explored the ethical and moral implications, especially in the case of AGIs and ASIs, and how an AI claiming self-awareness could raise massive ethical concerns.

This chapter also explored various classifications of AI systems, some obsolete, some new, and some hypothetical. We took a journey through the road map of AI development and learned how the next generation of AI systems would likely lead to an explosion of AI development.

We touched on the techniques we'll be using for training our ML-Agents in Unity and learned how combining these techniques will yield the best results.

We then wrapped up this chapter by discussing various practical use cases for Unity ML-Agents.

In the next chapter, we'll look into reinforcement learning and how it uses rewards to optimize for the best outcome.

CHAPTER 4

Dopamine for Machines

In this chapter, we'll be discussing the reward system used in reinforcement learning agents and how the reinforcement learning system took inspiration from the biological reward system that drives humanity and many other organisms found on earth.

We'll talk about how these reward systems work in biological organisms and then look at how engineers have taken inspiration from the reward system and implemented it into reinforcement learning agents for incredible results.

Then you'll learn how and when to reward your ML-Agents and various techniques for creating reliable training plans for your agents.

We'll look into how various approaches to rewards impact training time and overall performance of the ML-Agent.

Finally, you'll learn how to take the reward system further by enabling team-based rewards for agents.

Team-based rewards allow your ML-Agents to cooperate toward a common goal while each agent is capable of having completely separate subgoals.

This chapter is exciting and will wrap up the preliminary introduction. From there, we'll start digging into the ML-Agents package itself.

© Dylan Engelbrecht 2023
D. Engelbrecht, *Introduction to Unity ML-Agents*,
https://doi.org/10.1007/978-1-4842-8998-3_4

Dopamine

Dopamine (Figure 4-1) is a neurotransmitter in the brain's regions responsible for the "reward system."

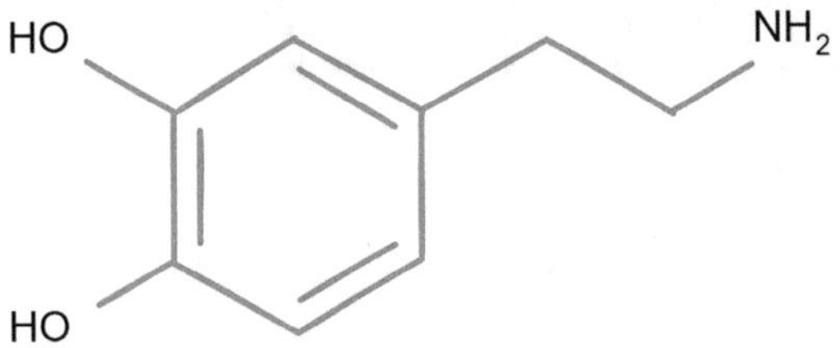

Figure 4-1. *The chemical structure of dopamine*

The current consensus with pharmacologists is that dopamine is responsible for signaling the perceived motivational prominence of an outcome to the brain.

This perceived motivational prominence means dopamine encourages or discourages a particular perceived outcome and drives us away or into doing things.

This reward system is not exclusive to humans; many animals and organisms typically have a reward system.

Other animals that have a reward system include dogs and mice.

Let's look at how humans use dopamine as a signal and how our reward system works.

Dopamine in Humans

Dopamine plays a vital part in the reward system within the human brain. This system drives the desire or craving for reward and motivation.

The reward system is also responsible for positive reinforcement learning and classical conditioning.

A reward is essentially the motivational and attractive property of a stimulus that encourages what's known as approach behavior and consummatory behavior.

The brain's reward mechanism is vital to animal survival and evolution.

Many associate the word dopamine with pleasure, but that's not necessarily the case.

And more so, "reward" is often associated with "pleasure."

However, the reward itself does not necessarily imply pleasure.

To better understand how we use rewards in reinforcement learning, it's essential to take a deeper look at how reward works in humans.

There are two types of rewards in a broad sense.

The first, which you may be more familiar with, is a naturally pleasurable stimulus and, therefore, attractive to the brain – an intrinsic reward.

Intrinsic rewards are inherently pleasurable and cause a response from the pleasure center in the brain.

Not all rewards are intrinsic. Many confuse all rewards as intrinsic, but that's not the case.

Many non-intrinsic rewards are confused with intrinsic rewards because we have conditioned ourselves to receive pleasure from them.

That leads us to the second type of reward, extrinsic rewards.

Extrinsic rewards are rewarding due to a learned association with a given intrinsic reward.

In machine learning, we lean heavily on this principle to build agents that can make associations to actions with intrinsic rewards.

This approach allows us to define the reward scheme and allows the AI to associate actions with rewards, creating extrinsic rewards.

By allowing AI to build up its extrinsic rewards, build AI agents capable of fulfilling the goal that we give it in the form of a reward scheme.

In humans, a different system could be a part of the reward system, the antireward system, proposed by Koob and Le Moal.

It could explain why humans will not get stuck into the same task indefinitely, acting as the brake system for the reward system.

We might see such a system implemented into reinforcement learning systems to help push them toward general intelligence.

The reward system in animals shares many similarities with that of humans.

Dopamine in Animals

While I wish I could tell you that our reward system is far more advanced than animals, I can't – the human reward system shares many traits with animals.

Modern humans are new at an evolutionary scale, and our reward systems are similar to what early humans would have had.

The only difference is that humans can leverage their understanding of reward to bend it.

Animals, on the other hand, can't.

Because animals are bound to their reward system, it makes some of them easy to train or domesticate.

We can leverage an animal's lack of sentience to condition them.

Conditioning is a process in which we give an animal new extrinsic rewards by having them act and then associating that action with an intrinsic reward.

The process for training animals is similar to that of current reinforcement learning techniques.

This process of creating new extrinsic rewards brings us to our next topic, dopamine in machines.

Dopamine in Machines

Reinforcement learning takes heavy inspiration from the reward system. In machines, we represent intrinsic reward as a floating-point value and then program the AI agent to optimize its actions to achieve the highest "reward" value.

An AI engineer aims to define training and reward structures that result in the most performant neural network models.

To train an ML-Agent, we create a training environment for it.

In this training environment, we give rewards based on the performance of the ML-Agent.

Our goal is to have the ML-Agent associate these intrinsic rewards with actions that we deem beneficial to the training and, as a result, form extrinsic rewards, much like human and animal brains.

We then give the ML-Agent access to various inputs.

These inputs can be a variety of different things, from

- Floating-point values

- Integer values

- Arrays of values

- Complex data structures such as raw images

- Booleans

The AI then interprets this data as inputs.

It's worth noting that many ML algorithms normalize these values, but you can often experience better results if you do this normalization.

From there, the AI observes these inputs during the observation phase.

We can then request a decision from the AI. What this does is query the ML-Agent to act in the form of output.

Much like inputs, outputs can also contain various data types and structures.

In Unity ML-Agents, we receive these outputs in the form of a method, with the actual values stored within an argument of type:

```
public override void OnActionReceived(ActionBuffers
actionBuffers)
```

We'll dig into the code in a future chapter. We can access these actionBuffers to receive the ML-Agent's intent.

What happens is that an ML-Agent receives a decision request from us.

Based on the observations that it's made, it then gives us back a set of action buffers. This flow is shown in Figure 4-2.

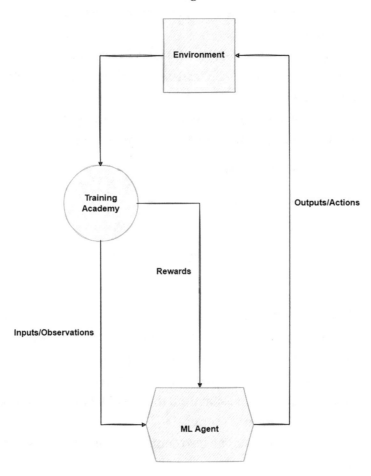

Figure 4-2. *The ML-Agents training loop*

Then, depending on our reward logic, we reward the ML-Agent based on how well that decision impacted the progress of the AI toward the goal we have in mind.

The ML-Agent then interprets these rewards and forms extrinsic rewards based on the outputs it provides, given a set of inputs or observations.

This training reinforces behavior that increases the intrinsic reward value, and over time the ML-Agent improves at the given goal until, if trained correctly, it far exceeds human capability.

Let's discuss how we can train ML-Agents.

Training Reinforcement Learning Agents

To train our ML-Agent, we first need to set up what's known as a training environment. This environment is essentially the scene that we use for training the ML-Agents.

A training environment then consists of at least one training area.

We typically set up a training area as a self-contained area where one or more agents train.

We then duplicate the training area as often as possible until our hardware bottlenecks the training process.

This approach allows us to parallelize the training workload to speed up training times significantly.

Then we plan out how we want our agent to work; it needs to

- Perceive the world using inputs

- Have a way to act on requested decisions

- Be rewarded for its actions if those actions benefit its goals

The next step is to establish rewards for the given goal. We'll go into more detail on how to set up rewards shortly.

For example, suppose the agent's goal is to reach a target point. In that case, we can decide to reward it whenever it arrives at the target destination, moves toward the target destination, or a hybrid of both, then finally reset the state of the training area.

However, figuring out the right reward system is a large part of the challenge of developing ML-Agents.

Suppose we were to reward a target whenever it moves toward a target destination; it might discover that it gets more reward by moving toward the target and then away from the target as many times as possible.

We could solve this loophole by penalizing the agent whenever it moves away from the target destination.

That sounds great in theory, but what happens when obstacles are in the way? Obstacles that require the agent to move away from the target temporarily?

In such a case, you may be better off only rewarding the target when reaching the destination. However, in this situation, the ML-Agent may never know that it gets rewarded when reaching the goal.

So perhaps you can use the two approaches together.

These are all things to consider when designing your reward structure. Let's take a deeper look into how and when you should reward your ML-Agents.

How and When to Reward Your ML-Agents

Deciding when to reward your ML-Agent forms the basis of a reward strategy.

You should plan and draft a design specification document describing your ML-Agent's goal.

Creating a design specification will allow you to break the task down and provide insights into how the ML-Agent may struggle given a particular reward system.

You should aim to reward your AI whenever it performs an action that will push it in the direction of completing the goal.

However, this is easier said than done. If you make your reward structure too rigid, the AI may never find unanticipated and potentially better approaches to the challenge.

Inversely, if the reward structure is not strict enough, you risk having the AI perform poorly.

So the goal is to create an intuitive reward structure that encourages extrinsic reward creation where needed.

The thing to remember, though, is that a reward doesn't always have to be a positive value. An AI making a poor decision will have real-world consequences in real-world applications.

Because of this, we can also assign a negative value to the reward, essentially a penalty.

Suppose our ML-Agent had to avoid touching a particular obstacle on the way to its target. In this situation, we may wish to assign a negative reward value to the ML-Agent whenever it makes a collision with an obstacle.

Or perhaps, the scenario that we're training it for requires that it never touches an obstacle, avoiding it at all costs.

In such a situation, we can give a sizeable negative reward to the agent and end the current training iteration.

This harsh negative reward and ending of the training iteration has a twofold effect.

Firstly, the ML-Agent receives a massively lower training score for the training iteration. Secondly, the ML-Agent cannot increase their score further for that training iteration.

This approach results in overall poor scores for the training iteration and encourages the ML-Agent to perform better by indirectly creating an extrinsic reward for avoiding obstacles.

This extrinsic reward will form as the ML-Agent starts associating the action of colliding with the obstacle as a massive reward.

Another situation that one might consider is time limitations.

Suppose the use case requires the ML-Agent to perform the task as fast as possible without colliding with obstacles.

We could add a time limit to the training iteration, but this might not be the best approach.

This approach would be unideal because when the AI starts training, it will take a long time to figure out what it needs to do – to form those extrinsic rewards to achieve the desired goal.

So it may never have enough time to reach the destination, resulting in poor training and overall poor results.

Instead, we could incentivize speed by altering the reward for the final destination based on the time taken.

This way, the ML-Agent may associate the speed of task completion with a better reward, thus creating an extrinsic reward for performing the task quickly and effectively.

And that brings me to my next point, "a sound reward system makes for great ML-Agents."

A Sound Reward System Makes for Great ML-Agents

To create great ML-Agents, you must plan out a solid reward system that will encourage the formation of beneficial extrinsic rewards that the agent can use to achieve its intended goal.

When training an ML-Agent, there are some significant factors to consider. Some of these include

- Training time

- ML-Agent effectiveness and overall complexity

Let's talk about training time first concerning the reward structure.

How Reward Systems Influence Training Time

There are many influencers of training time when building ML-Agents.

When creating your ML-Agent, a sound reward system will allow your ML-Agents to reach their goal and rapidly improve throughout the training process.

If you fail at this step, your agent may struggle – or outright fail – at achieving its intended goal.

If this is the case, your training process could run for hours, days, or weeks without notable improvements in agent decision-making.

So you must ensure that you build the reward system to advance the ML-Agent's progress.

Once that's done and your training is running, you may notice that it's still taking a long time.

You may have heard, "One woman can deliver a baby in nine months, but nine women can't deliver a baby in one month." Well, thankfully, in the world of AI, they can.

We can duplicate the training areas to provide parallelized training to the agents, exponentially increasing the speed at which we train the neural network.

This parallelization means that nine training areas would train at roughly nine times the speed of a single training area.

So what we want to do at this step is to increase the number of training areas to the point where our physical hardware becomes the bottleneck.

The second factor we should consider when training ML-Agents is how appropriate the ML-Agent is for the given goal.

The ML-Agent's training time and ability are significantly affected by its effectiveness for a given goal.

For some goals, you may be better off using a traditional software solution to a problem.

You should constantly evaluate if a traditional software approach makes more sense for a given goal, but we are here to learn about ML-Agents.

So let's discuss various aspects of rewarding and punishing an ML-Agent.

Various Aspects of Rewarding and Punishing ML-Agents

As we discussed, ML-Agents use a model-based reinforcement learning approach, so we need to ensure that the agent has reward signals that ultimately lead to them solving and optimizing their approach to achieving the desired goal.

There are two parts to this:

- Positive reinforcement

- Negative reinforcement

And we should use these two parts together to achieve the best results.

In positive reinforcement, we reward the ML-Agent when it acts with the desired outcome.

And inversely, we use a negative reward to penalize the ML-Agent for acting with an undesirable outcome.

When planning your reward system, it's essential to give the ML-Agent as much leniency as possible without giving it too much leniency.

Being too lenient on an ML-Agent may prevent it from achieving the desired outcome.

As I explained earlier, you may have an ML-Agent required to reach a given destination.

In such a situation, if you penalize the agent for moving away from the target, it may never understand that moving around an obstacle is desired.

In some situations, a step backward is two steps forward.

If you have too many negative rewards, you will limit the ML-Agent's curiosity and ability to find new solutions to a given problem.

However, suppose you have a situation where you are training an ML-Agent to drive a car. In this situation, colliding with an obstacle should be avoided.

You want to ensure that the ML-Agent is significantly penalized if it performs an action that would cause a harmful outcome to the training.

So far, we've discussed training a single ML-Agent, but that's not all the ML-Agents package can do. We can even train ML-Agents to function in a team, all while serving niche roles within the group!

This training structure means we have team-based ML-Agents with role-specific reward structures while contributing to a team.

Let's briefly look at team-based rewards before exploring them in depth later in the book.

Team-Based Rewards

Team-based rewards are, quite literally, rewards based on teamwork.

They are rewards that we give to agents within a group of agents working toward a common goal.

Team-based learning opens up new training possibilities because we can reward team agents differently based on their roles within the group.

Yet they will still share in rewards based on the team's outcomes.

In team-based learning, a team can consist of multiple ML-Agents sharing a brain – a multiagent group.

Then each agent in a multiagent group is configured with reward structures relevant to its role.

Finally, each agent in the group is given a shared reward structure in conjunction with its existing reward structure.

So that if one agent performs a beneficial task, all agents in the group receive some reward.

This approach allows agents to require getting better but enforces extrinsic rewards for helping the team complete the primary goal.

Conclusion

This chapter was exciting. We learned how human and animal brains have heavily inspired reinforcement learning techniques.

We learned the difference between intrinsic and extrinsic rewards and how these play a significant part in reinforcement learning.

We also discussed the importance of good reward structure planning and explored various aspects of when to reward ML-Agents for achieving optimal results.

Finally, we wrapped up this chapter by touching on multiagent groups and team-based reinforcement learning.

In the next chapter, we'll set up all of the prerequisites for ML-Agents and configure our starting project.

CHAPTER 5

ML-Agents Setup

In this chapter, we'll go through the setup process required on both the Unity and the Python sides.

On the Unity side of things, I'll show you how to create a new project or open the example project you can find in this book.

Then on the Python side, we'll go through the setup process for Pycharm Community Edition. You will also learn how to create a virtual environment (venv), where we will install PyTorch and its dependencies.

From there, we'll go back to Unity and install the ML-Agents package, ML-Agents extensions, and ML-Agents samples.

We'll then validate our configuration against one of the Unity ML-Agents samples to confirm that we correctly installed and configured our project and are ready for development before we build our ML-Agents in the next chapter.

To get the most out of ML-Agents, you should already have a good understanding of Unity. However, I will be somewhat accommodating to those who may be unfamiliar with Unity.

We'll begin with the Unity setup.

Unity Setup

You should already be familiar with the Unity setup process; if not, you can download it from the following URL:

```
https://unity3d.com/get-unity/download
```

© Dylan Engelbrecht 2023
D. Engelbrecht, *Introduction to Unity ML-Agents*,
https://doi.org/10.1007/978-1-4842-8998-3_5

Follow the Unity Hub setup instructions and install version 2021.3.x LTS of the Unity Editor.

There are two ways to follow along with this project:

- By creating a new project using the built-in render pipeline and installing the official ML-Agents package and then copying the samples from this book's repository

- By cloning the example repository which contains a project preconfigured with Unity ML-Agents and the ML-Agents extensions

Let's start by creating a new project in the following section.

If you would like to clone the example repository with the preconfigured project, then you can skip the new project setup and move on to the "Opening the Example GitHub Project" section.

New Project Setup

In your Unity Editor, create a new project **using Unity Version 2021.3.8f1 and the built-in render pipeline**. You will want to use the "3D – Core" template for this, as in Figure 5-1.

Figure 5-1. *The template to be selected for installing a fresh project*

Once done, you can go ahead and open up your new project.

In preparation for the ML-Agents package, we will need to update your new project to use the new Input System.

Installing the new Input System will prevent you from encountering many errors in your console when importing the Unity ML-Agents package.

To do this, navigate to "**Window ➤ Package Manager**" again and search the Unity Registry for "**Input System**."

Go ahead and install the new Input System. I will be using version 1.4.2.

Unity will then prompt you to restart the editor. Accept this prompt and wait for your Unity Editor to relaunch.

You can use the image in Figure 5-2 for reference.

Figure 5-2. *The Unity Input System package*

If you are updating an existing project that uses the old Input System with dependent code, you can set Active Input Handling to both in Edit ➤ Project Settings ➤ Player ➤ Other Settings.

You're now ready to move on and install the Unity ML-Agents package!

ML-Agents Unity Package Setup

To install ML-Agents, we're going to install it using the package manager. Unity ML-Agents is a package within the package manager.

We will be installing the following package:

- Name: **com.unity.ml-agents**

- Version: **2.2.1-exp.1**

Version 2.2.1-exp.1 is experimental, but contains many fixes since the current release version of 2.0.1.

1) Start by opening your Unity project. From here, you want to go to the toolbar at the top of Unity and navigate to

   Window ➤ Package Manager

   Unity will then open the package manager window.

2) Select the + icon from the package manager window at the window's top-right.

   The icon will expand with additional options. Select "**Add package by name...**" from this dropdown.
   You can see this in Figure 5-3.

Figure 5-3. *The add package by name dialog*

3) From here, we will install the exact version that I am using for this book. So fill in the relevant fields with the following information:

   - Name: **com.unity.ml-agents**

   - Version: **2.2.1-exp.1**

Then start the installation process by clicking **Add**.

Congratulations, you've successfully installed the ML-Agents core package.

Installing the ML-Agents Extensions Package

The next step is installing the official ML-Agents extensions package, which contains various additional experimental sensors we can use to build our ML-Agents.

1) To access the Unity ML-Agents extensions package, we'll need to open our package manager window again.

2) From here, click the large "+" icon at the top left of the window.

Then select "**Add package from git URL**" which will prompt you to enter a value.

In this value box, enter the following URL without any spaces or line breaks:

git+https://github.com/Unity-Technologies/ml-agents. git?path=com.unity.ml-agents.extensions#release_19

Follow this step by clicking the "**Add**" button.

The Unity package manager will begin installing the extensions from the official ML-Agents repository.

This step may take a while, and Unity does not display a progress bar.

You can validate that the files are undergoing installation by selecting "**Packages - Other, Adding a new package**."

The package manager will then confirm that it is installing the files. You can see this in Figure 5-4.

Figure 5-4. *How to install the official ML-Agents extensions*

Once completed, a new package will appear under the "**Packages - Other**" category.

This package will be titled "**ML Agents Extensions**."

You now have the ML-Agents core package, as well as its extensions.

The next step from here is to install the Python requirements. However, I will first cover how to open the example project built for this book.

Even if you opted to set up your project from scratch, I am still going to highly recommend following the next section.

Opening the Example GitHub Project

This book has a GitHub repository containing samples of the work we will do throughout the rest of the book.

The example project contains the code that this book will discuss; it is highly recommended that you do not skip this step.

You can find the GitHub repository at the following link:

`https://github.com/apress/introduction-unity-ml-agents`

If you encounter any issues with the sample project, you are more than welcome to open an issue request on GitHub, and I'll be sure to get to it.

I will also be covering the creation of GitHub issues.

1) The first step is to install a Git client of your choice. I'll cover GitHub Desktop, as it's free and straightforward.

   You can download GitHub Desktop from the following URL:
   https://desktop.github.com/
   Then click the download button (Figure 5-5) to begin the setup process.

Figure 5-5. *Where to download GitHub Desktop*

2) Once downloaded, proceed with the setup process on the screen.

   There are also some great alternatives to GitHub Desktop.
   Although they typically have a price tag, they are worth it in environments where you will be interacting with Git frequently:

   • JetBrains Rider IDE Github Support – My personal preference

   • www.jetbrains.com/rider/

- GitKraken

- www.gitkraken.com/

- Fork

- https://git-fork.com/

Once you've installed your Git client of choice, the next step is to clone the repository, fork it, or download it as a zip. I will cover the process of cloning the repository, as that will allow you to receive updates from the book's repository.

The alternatives are to fork the repository and then clone the fork, which copies the repository to your GitHub account.

The other option is to download the repository as a zip file, which I would advise against, as you would lose the benefits of receiving updates that I release. At this point, you should have GitHub Desktop installed and open.

3) Open the GitHub repository page at the following URL:
   https://github.com/apress/introduction-unity-ml-agents

4) From the GitHub repository page, click the green "**Code**" button with the dropdown arrow and select "**Open with GitHub Desktop**."
   You can see where to click in Figure 5-6.

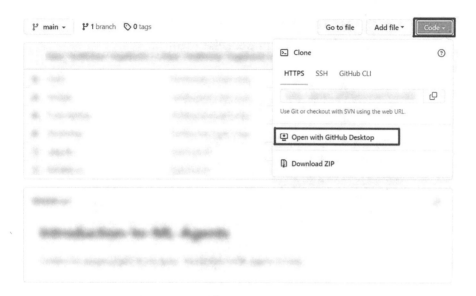

Figure 5-6. *How to open the repository in GitHub Desktop*

5) This action will prompt your browser to ask you for permission to open GitHub Desktop (Figure 5-7). You can accept this request, and GitHub Desktop will open.

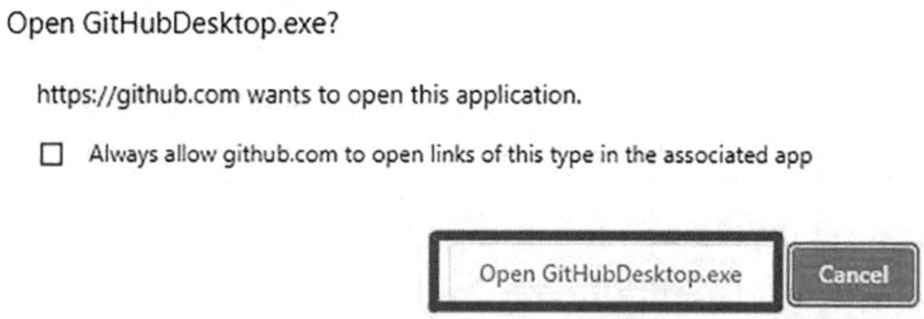

Open GitHubDesktop.exe?

https://github.com wants to open this application.

☐ Always allow github.com to open links of this type in the associated app

Open GitHubDesktop.exe   Cancel

Figure 5-7. *The permission prompt that the browser will display, requesting permission to open GitHub Desktop*

6) Once GitHub Desktop gets the request from the browser, GitHub Desktop will prefill the required

settings to clone the repository. From here, you can select the destination folder (Figure 5-8).

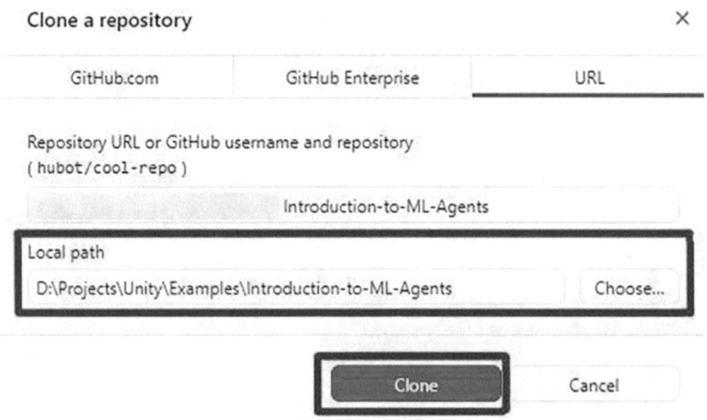

Figure 5-8. *The "clone a repository" prompt in GitHub Desktop*

Great! You've now successfully cloned the repository page for the book. However, you still don't have the files.

If you're unfamiliar with the Git protocol, it has several concepts you should learn.

The most notable of those is "**Commit**," "**Push**," and "**Pull**." Since you won't be modifying the repository, the one you'll primarily use is "**Pull**."

Commit

This process is where you mark changes you would like to submit for change recording to your local device.

The action of committing does not send the files to the repository. Instead, it marks them for sending and allows you to attach a message describing your changes.

Think of it like gift wrapping a present with a card before giving it to someone.

Push

Pushing is the action of sending your commits to the repository.

This action sends the files to the remote repository, like the action of giving someone the present that you wrapped.

Pull/Fetch

Pull, also referred to as fetch, is the process of requesting and retrieving the latest files on the remote repository.

As we discussed, you have cloned the repository but have yet to request and retrieve the files from the remote repository.

To do that, click the "**Fetch Origin**" button at the top right of your GitHub Desktop, as shown in Figure 5-9.

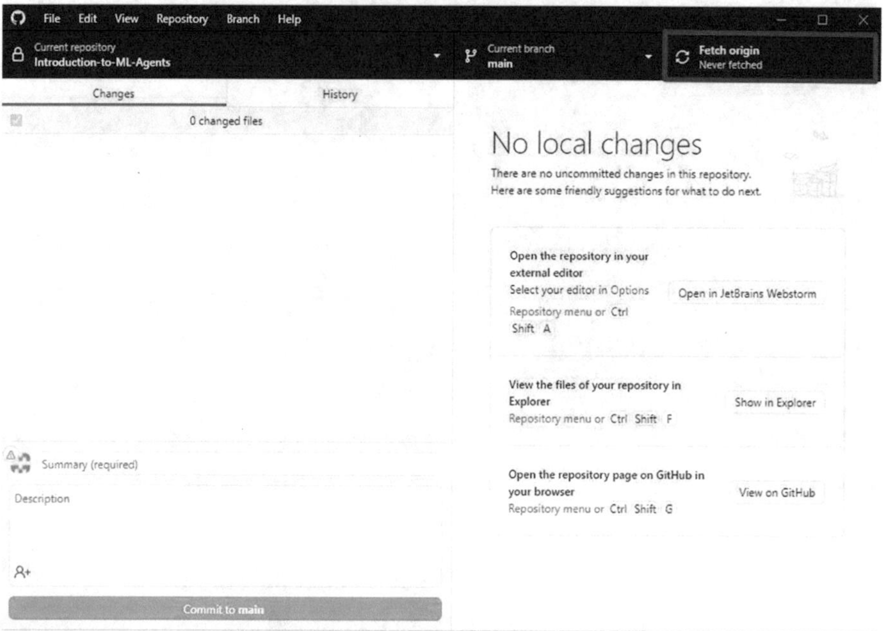

*Figure 5-9. How to "**Fetch Origin**" in GitHub Desktop*

Pulling or fetching will start downloading the files from the remote repository.

7)   Now we're ready to open the project in Unity! Go
ahead, open your Unity Hub, and then navigate to
the "**Projects**" tab.

The next step is to click the "**Open**" button at the top
right (Figure 5-10).

Figure 5-10. *How to open the repository in Unity Hub*

8)   Unity Hub will then prompt you to choose a folder.
Point this prompt to wherever you cloned the
repository.

Once completed, your Unity will detect the repository folder as a
project and open the Unity Editor.

Congratulations, you now have access to the example project for
the book.

Let's discuss opening issues on GitHub.

Creating a GitHub Issue

While we've tested the examples, there is always the possibility of encountering issues. Thankfully, GitHub has a built-in issue tracker.

This issue tracker allows you to raise bugs or ask questions.

These bugs and questions are then viewable by me or someone else in the community, which is a great way to get help specific to this book.

If you're unfamiliar with GitHub, this section will cover creating these issue tickets.

1) The first step is to go to the book's GitHub issue page at the following URL:
   `https://github.com/apress/introduction-unity-ml-agents/issues`

2) Then click the "New Issue" button on the right (Figure 5-11).

Figure 5-11. *How to create a new issue*

Creating a new issue will allow you to insert a title for your problem and a description.

Please remember to include a detailed description and a relevant title to make it easier for the community and me to help you out.

3) Once you're happy with the information provided, click the "**Submit New Issue**" button at the bottom right.

   See Figure 5-12 for an example.

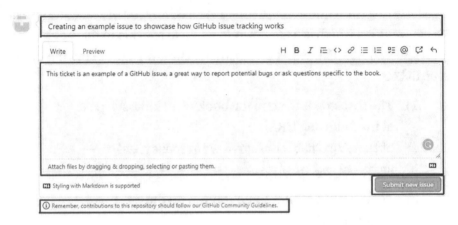

Figure 5-12. *How to open the repository in Unity Hub*

Once done, GitHub will take you to your new issue and automatically subscribe you to listen for activity on the issue. The example issue looks like Figure 5-13.

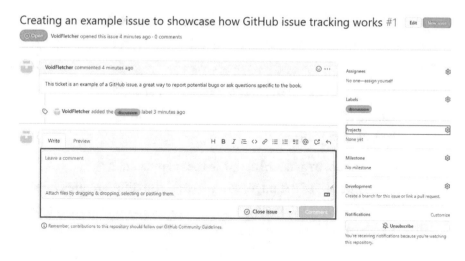

Figure 5-13. *Your newly created GitHub issue*

Now that we have a Unity project, ideally by both having created a new project and cloned the example project for the book, we can move on to the next step.

The next step is configuring Python with all the relevant ML-Agents requirements.

Python Setup

Unity ML-Agents requires the use of PyTorch.

PyTorch is the open source Python machine learning framework that powers our neural networks. ML-Agents is a wrapper for this framework, and PyTorch is what handles the creation of the underlying neural network.

So while we'll do most of the work with ML-Agents, we still need a working installation of PyTorch so that ML-Agents can create our agent.

We'll need to install and configure Python and the various packages necessary for PyTorch and Unity ML-Agents.

For our Python setup, we'll be targeting **Python 3.7.9** due to its stability, and the team at Unity has tested it thoroughly for their ML-Agents package.

1) You can download **Python 3.7.9**, the latest stable 3.7 release with the latest installer as of this writing, at the following URL:

   `www.python.org/downloads/release/python-379/`
   At the bottom of the page, you will find the different files for this release. We are interested in the 64-bit executable installer, titled "`Windows x86-64 executable installer`."
   Figure 5-14 highlights where you can click to download the correct installer.

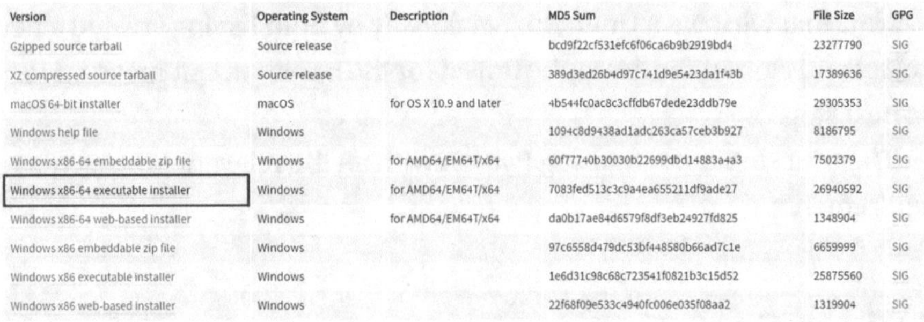

Version	Operating System	Description	MD5 Sum	File Size	GPG
Gzipped source tarball	Source release		bcd9f22cf531efc6f06ca6b9b2919bd4	23277790	SIG
XZ compressed source tarball	Source release		389d3ed26b4d97c741d9e5423da1f43b	17389636	SIG
macOS 64-bit installer	macOS	for OS X 10.9 and later	4b544fc0ac8c3cffdb67dede23ddb79e	29305353	SIG
Windows help file	Windows		1094c8d9438ad1adc263ca57ceb3b927	8186795	SIG
Windows x86-64 embeddable zip file	Windows	for AMD64/EM64T/x64	60f77740b30030b22699dbd14883a4a3	7502379	SIG
Windows x86-64 executable installer	Windows	for AMD64/EM64T/x64	7083fed513c3c9a4ea655211df9ade27	26940592	SIG
Windows x86-64 web-based installer	Windows	for AMD64/EM64T/x64	da0b17ae84d6579f8df3eb24927fd825	1348904	SIG
Windows x86 embeddable zip file	Windows		97c6558d479dc53bf448580b66ad7c1e	6659999	SIG
Windows x86 executable installer	Windows		1e6d31c98c68c723541f0821b3c15d52	25875560	SIG
Windows x86 web-based installer	Windows		22f68f09e533c4940fc006e035f08aa2	1319904	SIG

Figure 5-14. *The installer for 64-bit Windows*

2) Now that you have the install file, you can run it. As with the other installs, the process is quite straightforward; however, I would *highly recommend* checking the box "`Add Python 3.7 to PATH`" (Figure 5-15).

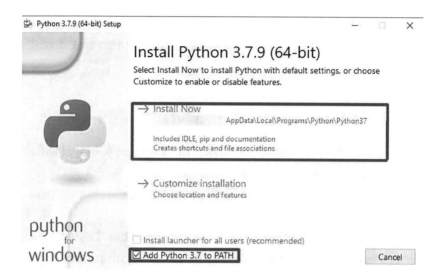

Figure 5-15. *The checkbox that allows Python to install to Windows PATH*

This action will add it to your Windows PATH, allowing you to type Python commands into your Windows command prompt. It's worth noting that this will require a restart of your PC.

3) Once you've installed Python, added it to PATH, and restarted your PC, open the Windows command prompt by pressing the Windows key + R, then typing "cmd".

Doing this will bring up your Windows command prompt. From here, type the following command:

python -version

If installed correctly, it should display "Python 3.7.9" in which case your setup was successful. There are, however, still a few things we need to do.

We need to install all of the required packages for ML-Agents, and to keep things manageable, we'll set up what's known as a virtual environment.

Creating a Virtual Environment

Installing many different packages can get messy when you deal with multiple Python projects unrelated to ML-Agents.

It gets messy because, by default, all packages would install in the same place.

So, we use a virtual environment to keep our work and Python installations organized. I'll be installing my virtual environment in the following directory:

/Introduction-to-ML-Agents/VirtualEnvironment/

Due to GitHub repository size restrictions, the project repository will not include the final installed ML-Agent files in this directory. However, you can still proceed with the same project structure. You can safely move this folder after you have followed these steps if you need to:

1) Head over to the Unity project directory to create the virtual environment, **often referred to as venv**.

2) The next step is to open a command prompt terminal in the Unity project folder or wherever else you'd like to install your virtual environment.

   The quickest way to do this is to open your Windows file explorer and navigate to the folder, click the address bar, type "**cmd**", and press enter as shown in Figure 5-16.

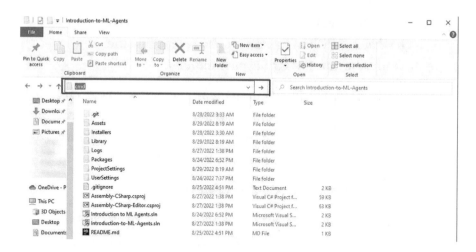

Figure 5-16. *How to open the command prompt in a directory*

3) Once your command prompt is open in the project directory, we're ready to start with the virtual environment setup.

   In your command prompt, execute the following command:

   python -m venv VirtualEnvironment

   The format for this is "**python -m venv [Virtual Environment Name]**".
   So you can give yours a different name if you would like, or name yours "**VirtualEnvironment**".
   The benefit of naming it the same as me is that the process would be easier to follow.

4) Now, you should have a folder with your virtual environment setup. The folder should also contain a new **Scripts** folder.

   /Introduction-to-ML-Agents/VirtualEnvironment/Scripts/

5)   The next step is to activate the virtual environment
      so that our Python commands execute within the
      context of our new virtual environment.

      To do this, go to your command prompt terminal currently open
      in your virtual environment's parent directory. In this example,
      it is open within the context of the Unity project directory. Then
      execute the following command:

      VirtualEnvironment\Scripts\activate

      If you've done this correctly, venv should now prefix your
      terminal input line with "**(VirtualEnvironment)**" followed by
      the directory.
      Your virtual environment is now active on this terminal. You
      must execute the activate command whenever you want to work
      in this virtual environment.
      If this sounds tedious, if you've cloned the example project,
      you'll be delighted that I've included a batch file in the **/
      VirtualEnvironment** folder named "**ml-agents-terminal.bat**"
      which you can move to your virtual environment folder.
      You can use this batch file to activate and deactivate the virtual
      environment.

6)   Once you activate your virtual environment, we can
      proceed to the next step.

      Next, we need to ensure that you're running an up-to-date
      version of Pip3.
      Pip3 is the official package manager for Python version 3.X – we
      can use it to install and manage various Python packages.

7)   **Before installing, if you have a highly aggressive
      third-party antivirus, I suggest temporarily
      disabling live shields during the following setup
      steps, as this may interrupt your installation.**

8)   To upgrade pip3 to the latest, run the following
command inside your venv:

```
py -m pip install --upgrade pip
```

8.1) If you encounter the following error:
ModuleNotFoundError: No module named 'pip'
Then you can run the following command instead:

```
py -m ensurepip --upgrade
```

followed by rerunning the previous command.

You now have Python, Python's package manager, and a virtual environment.

The next step is to start installing our dependencies.

Installing ML-Agents and Dependencies

We will need

- PyTorch

- ML-Agents

- ML-Agents dependencies

Let's start. We will need to install PyTorch **before** installing the ML-Agents packages.

1)   In your venv, execute the following command in one
line, using a single space after the **-f** followed by the
URL. If you intend to copy the following command
instead of writing it out, then I would suggest
copying this command to notepad or another text
editor and then copying it again before pasting it
into the terminal to avoid line break issues.

```
pip3 install torch~=1.7.1 -f https://download.pytorch.
org/whl/torch_stable.html
```

This command will download and install PyTorch and all its dependencies.

1.1) **The command WILL NOT WORK unless you have EXACTLY Python 3.7.9 as your primary Python installation.**

1.2) If your `python --version` command does not say version 3.7.9, you will need to uninstall all other versions of Python or modify your Windows PATH variable.

2) Next, we're ready to install the **ML-Agents** package. To do this, you'll want to execute the following command in your venv:

```
py -m pip install mlagents==0.28.0
```

This command will download and install the ML-Agents Python package and its dependencies. You may see a sizeable list of warnings during the setup process.
However, these are not critical.

3) Finally, you can validate that you successfully installed your ML-Agents Python package by executing the following command within your venv:

```
mlagents-learn --help
```

If your installation was successful, this command should print out a long list of commands.
That's it for the Python installation.

4) If you disabled your antivirus shields for the installation, please remember to reenable your shields.

We can now proceed with finalizing our Python setup, by validating that everything is working.

Validating Our ML-Agents Installation with Samples

We can validate our ML-Agents installation by copying the official ML-Agents examples into your project. If you've cloned the repository for this book, then you will not need to download them again and can find them in the directory of the example project listed as follows:

Introduction-to-ML-Agents\Assets\ML-Agents\Examples

1) If you're following along in your own project, then be sure to copy that folder into your project's "**Assets**" folder in such a way that the directory tree matches.

    Your project's "**Assets**" folder should align with that of the book's example project.
    This means that you should copy **\ML-Agents\Examples** into your project's **\Assets** directory.
    Alternatively, you can download the latest official examples from the official ML-Agents repository using the following GitHub URL:
    https://github.com/Unity-Technologies/ml-agents/tree/main/Project/Assets/ML-Agents/Examples

2) Let's begin our testing by opening the 3DBall sample. In the Unity project window, navigate to and open the following file:

..\Assets\ML-Agents\Examples\3DBall\Scenes\3DBall.unity

You should now see a bunch of blue cubes stacked in a grid formation.

3) Click the Play button at the top of your editor window to start.

If all goes well, your little cube faces should be jiggling around to keep the ball from rolling off their heads.
If the cube people are moving, you have installed the ML-Agents package correctly and are currently running an ML-Agent with its trained model.
Your console should display a message saying that the trainer is not connected; this is fine and expected behavior, simply look to see if the cubes are moving at all.
These agents should look something like the image in Figure 5-17.

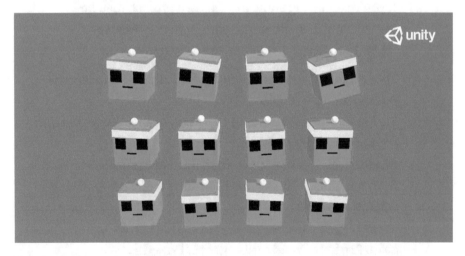

Figure 5-17. *The sample ML-Agents keeping a ball balanced on their head*

Well done!

Conclusion

You've successfully installed Python, ML-Agents, ML-Agents extensions, ML-Agents samples, and all the ML-Agents Python dependencies.

In the next chapter, we'll discuss ML-Agents in greater detail and start seeing how the concepts learned throughout the book apply in practice.

If you encounter issues with the example repository, please remember that you are more than welcome to raise a GitHub issue on the book's GitHub page.

CHAPTER 6

Unity ML-Agents

Now that we have a working installation of ML-Agents, we can take a more hands-on look at the system.

In this chapter, I'll discuss the various components of ML-Agents. We'll then discuss the learning environments inside the 3DBall sample scene, in which ML-Agents aim to balance a ball on their heads.

From here, we'll talk about inputs and outputs and get a better look at how our agent views the simulated world. Then we'll talk about rewards more practically and in depth than earlier in the book.

We'll pick apart the 3DBall sample, train the agent ourselves, and look at what saving and exporting an ML-Agent's neural network to a model file looks like.

Then we'll discuss how you can use the exported model by assigning it back to the agent for use.

We'll then wrap all of that up to reiterate what we've learned in the chapter. It will be a great chapter with a ton of learning.

ML-Agent Components

Let's begin by discussing the ML-Agent components that make up Unity ML-Agents.

I will be skimming over some concepts as right now we're just focused on knowing what's out there. I will go in depth into the various concepts later in the chapter.

D. Engelbrecht, *Introduction to Unity ML-Agents*,
https://doi.org/10.1007/978-1-4842-8998-3_6

We'll be opening the 3DBall official Unity ML-Agents sample scene as we did in the previous scene. You can find this scene in the following folder:

Assets/ML-Agents/Examples/3DBall/Scenes/3DBall.unity

Once your scene is open, select one of the "**3DBall**" objects in the scene hierarchy.

Then expand the "**3DBall**" object, and select the "**Agent**" object. The inspector window will now show you the components attached to the ML-Agents.

ML-Agents consist of three primary components:

- The behavior parameters

- The agent

- The decision requester

Let's start by discussing the **Behavior Parameters** component as shown in Figure 6-1.

Figure 6-1. *The behavior parameters component*

Behavior Parameters

In essence, this component determines the properties that dictate how the ML-Agent will run and configures the settings for the brain parameters and some additional settings like what device to use.

It's our glorified settings object.

Each behavior parameters component's field is vital to building a great ML-Agent.

Behavior Name

Let's start with the **Behavior Name** field.

The **Behavior Name**, as the name implies, is a field for a name for this behavior.

We use this name to identify the agent, and it should be unique unless the agents share the same functionality.

An important note is that you should never directly change the behavior name during runtime. Instead, you should use the following method on the behavior parameters component:

```
SetModel(string newName, NNModel newModel, InferenceDevice newDevice)
```

In typical situations, you can give your agent a meaningful name and leave it alone.

Vector Observations

Next, we have the vector observations.

The **Vector Observations** field tells the brain how many inputs to expect. It consists of **space size** and a **stacked vectors** count.

You must set the **space size** value to match the number of inputs your code gives the ML-Agent.

Let's presume I tell the agent to observe its current health and stamina – then we need to give a vector observation of 2 as the agent observes two float values.

A critical note is that you must break down complex types into float values. For example, if I tell it to monitor its current position, you need to set the vector observations to 3.

You need to set the value to 3 because a position is a Vector3 type consisting of three floats.

When collecting observations, we can pass in any of the following types, broken down into their respective floats:

- **float** – 1 vector observation

- **int** – 1 vector observation

- **bool** – 1 vector observation

- **Vector2** – 2 vector observations

- **Vector3** – 3 vector observations

- **IList<float>** – Length of list observations

- **Quaternion** – 4 observations

So depending on what types and how many observations you make, you need to calculate and set the **Space Size** field accordingly.

The next value is the **Stacked Vectors** field. The stacked vectors field tells the ML-Agent how far back in history it's capable of looking.

This ability to view past data can be helpful in some situations. However, it's important to note that the more stacked vectors you give your ML-Agent, the longer it will take to train.

In the following formula, we can see that if we had a space size of 10 and a stacked vector count of 5, we would have 50 total observations. This calculation means that the training performance of 50 total observations would be even slower than having an ML-Agent with a space size of 30 and a stacked vector count of 1, totaling 30 observations.

Space Size x Stacked Vectors = Total Observation Size

If you want to observe the direction of an entity, it may tempt you to have the ML-Agent monitor its position with a stacked vector size of 3. However, while the ML-Agent would be able to infer direction from this, you may be better off simply letting it observe the velocity.

So keep your total observations manageable, and you'll have agents that can train fast and efficiently.

Quicker training times mean shorter iteration time on improving your ML-Agent.

Actions

The actions field allows us to specify how many different continuous actions and discrete branches the agent should support.

Model

The model is the brain of the ML-Agent. It's a snapshot of the neurons formed and their weights.

The model field consists of three subfields:

- Model
- Inference device
- Deterministic interface

The model field takes in a model file we get when exporting a trained ML-Agent.

This model is what allows our ML-Agent to function, and we can serialize it and compile it into a build for runtime use.

Once we train an ML-Agent and generate the model, our ML-Agent performance improves significantly.

The inference device is the physical device the ML-Agent uses for inference.

The ML-Agent uses this device for runtime inference or playback of the model, not for the process of training.

So, for most situations, **Burst** is the most useful choice.

Next, we have the behavior type.

Behavior Type

There are three different **behavior types** that our behavior parameters component can take. These are

- Default

- HeuristicOnly

- InferenceOnly

The behavior type determines where the ML-Agent will make its decisions.

Default

Using **Default** as the behavior type will have the ML-Agent attempt to use the remote process, PyTorch, for decision-making.

If it's unable to use the remote process, it will fall back to using inference.

The ML-Agent will fall back to heuristic control if the inference is unavailable.

HeuristicOnly

This behavior type will always use heuristics. Heuristics is the mode where we provide manual actions to the neural network – in essence, making the decisions ourselves – typically through user input using Unity's Input System.

InferenceOnly

The inference-only behavior will always use inference on the provided model, which means that the agent will make decisions using the model by "inference."

Typically, a behavior type of **Default** is suitable for many situations unless you want to override the control. The next field on the behavior parameters is the **Team Id** field.

Team Id

The Team Id value specifies the team that the ML-Agent should contribute to, which is helpful for team-based ML-Agents.

Use Child Sensors

This checkbox allows us to tell the agent to find and use any sensors found through its own child hierarchy. This incurs a small performance impact, and you should keep this disabled unless you have child sensors on your agent.

Observable Attributes

Here, we can tell the agent if it should be using reflection to determine if the [Observable] attribute is in use. Using reflection incurs a large performance penalty, and if you are not using the attribute, then you should keep this disabled.

The Decision Requester

The decision requester is an optional component that requests a decision from the agent every **x** number of steps specified by the **DecisionPeriod** field. Let's take a look at the component in Figure 6-2.

Figure 6-2. *The decision requester component*

The decision requester is not needed if your agent implements
RequestDecision.

It has the following fields:

DecisionPeriod – This is the step interval to wait before making a new
decision on the attached agent.

TakeActionsBetweenDecisions – Specifies whether or not the agent
should take action between decisions on each academy step. If you set the
DecisionPeriod to **1**, this field will have no effect.

That's all the components you need on an agent to allow it to function;
however, there are additional components like sensors that we will discuss
later in the chapter.

Sensors are optional and are simply abstracted to allow for quickly
copying functionality between custom agents. That said, your agent is free
to implement a custom implementation of sensors.

We will cover this later in the chapter.

Next, let's look at learning environments and how we can group
multiple agents within the same scene to parallelize training, resulting in
significantly faster training times.

Learning Environments

Learning environments are isolated learning environments in which an
agent can train. As they are isolated, you can create many within the same
scene, typically via copy-paste, spacing them away from each other.

In Figure 6-3, let's look at how Unity Technologies created its learning
environments for its 3DBall sample.

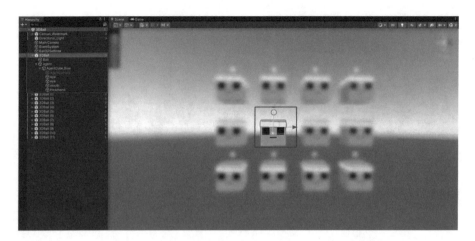

Figure 6-3. *The learning environment*

The learning environment in the **3DBall** sample consists of everything the agent needs to train. In this case, the agent and the ball that it needs to keep balanced on its head.

Unity developed this sample agent so that everything sits inside a single parent object, **3DBall**, that one can duplicate in the scene.

This way, the agent can train, regardless of whether it's a single agent or 100 agents.

In this case, we have 12 learning environments. It's important to point out that a learning environment is not a specific number of agents in a group – we define it as everything needed to train a model, ideally as a child of a single transform.

Let's take a sneak peek at one of the other samples to reinforce this concept of learning environments.

Figure 6-4 shows that of the SoccerTwos sample, which you can find under the path:

../Assets/ML-Agents/Examples/Soccer/SoccerTwos.unity

Let's take a look (Figure 6-4).

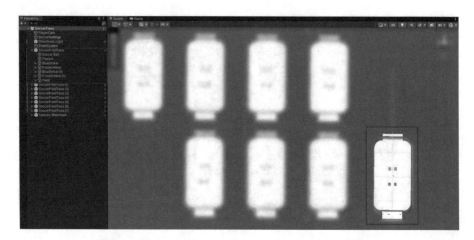

Figure 6-4. *The learning environment within the SoccerTwos sample*

This sample has four agents, goal posts, an environment, and a ball. We isolate everything into a learning environment. We then place it inside of a parent **gameobject** for easy copy-paste. We then duplicate the learning environment several times in the scene.

Again, we isolate everything we need to train a model. That is what makes a learning environment.

Now that we know what makes up an ML-Agent and its learning environment, let's dig deeper into how ML-Agents interpret and interact with the virtual world.

The Agent

The agent is the heart of your ML-Agent; it's where your code lives. As an example, in the official 3DBall example, our agent is of type **Ball3DAgent**.

We can see this in Figure 6-5.

Figure 6-5. *A custom implementation of the Agent class*

The only universal field on the agent is the MaxStep field, which determines how many academy steps an agent should complete before restarting.

You can set this to 0 for unlimited steps or until manually ending the episode.

To create an agent, you create a class that inherits from the **Agent** class. By inheriting from the **Agent** class, you can override several methods to build your agent.

Agent Override Methods

In this next section, we're going to be covering code elements.

If you would like to follow along with the code, switch back to the 3DBall scene.

You can then right-click the "Ball 3D Agent" component and select "Edit Script." However, Ball3DAgent does not implement everything; if you cannot find the corresponding method, do not be alarmed – we will cover more later in the chapter.

The goal right now is to see what's available.

Viewing the Ball3DAgent class will be a great way to see a few of the method overrides in use.

override void Initialize()

We'll start with the **Initialize** method.

You can override the **Initialize** method to do any first-time setup for your agent. The initialize method works much like the **Start** or **Awake** methods that **MonoBehaviour** classes provide – always prefer using "**Initialize**" over "**Start**" or "**Awake**."

override void CollectObservations(VectorSens or sensor)

Override the **CollectObservations** method to feed your ML-Agent observations.

Observations are data points representing the virtual world around the ML-Agent, and the agent can interpret this data into meaningful information about its environment and driving decisions.

We'll also cover observations in detail later in this chapter during the "Inputs and Outputs" section, so, for now, make a simple mental note that this is where observations happen.

override void OnActionReceived(ActionBuffers actionBuffers)

This method override is where decisions get turned into actions, and we implement the agent's actions. While this is an oversimplification, we'll also discuss this in detail during this chapter's "Inputs and Outputs" section.

So, for now, you can make a mental note that this is where our logic to interpret ML-Agent actions goes.

override void OnEpisodeBegin()

You should override the **OnEpisodeBegin** method and make it responsible for setting up your agent for a new training episode. You'll typically want to reset any cached values from a previous training episode or set any new values relevant to the latest training episode.

override void Heuristic(in ActionBuffers actionsOut)

Heuristics override allows us to choose actions for the ML-Agent. This method will enable us to set up the logic for that to occur. Heuristics are excellent for ensuring that our agent's base logic functions correctly, debugging, and imitation learning.

Next, we need a method to ask the ML-Agent to do something, and that's where the **RequestDecision** method comes in. Let's take a look.

The following methods we will discuss are not overriding, but are extremely important to training your ML-Agent. These methods include the add-and-set reward methods.

During the "Rewards" section later in this chapter, we will discuss rewards in detail, so don't get worried if you're feeling a little overwhelmed.

void RequestDecision()

You can call the **RequestDecision** method to tell the ML-Agent to make a decision. This functionality is much like the **DecisionRequester** component that we'll discuss shortly. However, it's important to note that if you use a **DecisionRequester** component, you should not call **RequestDecision** manually.

void AddReward(float increment)

AddRewards allows us to adjust the reward value for our agent's current episode incrementally. For the best results, you should almost only call this method during the OnActionsReceived method.

Positive reward values will reinforce behavior, and negative values discourage the behavior. Alternatively, you can set the reward instead of incrementing it using the SetReward method. Let's take a look at this next.

void SetReward(float reward)

Much like the AddReward method, SetReward adjusts the reward for the agent's current episode. The difference is that SetReward overrides the current value for the episode instead of updating it incrementally.

The next method to cover is the **EndEpisode** method.

void EndEpisode()

The EndEpisode method allows you to end the current episode and reset the agent, which is helpful in situations where an ML-Agent made a fatal mistake or achieved its goal.

The methods that we covered are the ones you're most likely to use.

With that said, there are several other methods for the agent class. I will touch on them briefly. They are as follows:

> **CollectDiscreteActionMasks(DiscreteAction Masker)** – Collects the masks for discrete actions, stopping the ML-Agent from using them during training and inference.
>
> **GetAction()** – Returns the last action decided upon by the agent without making a new decision.
>
> **GetCumulativeReward()** – Gets the total reward accumulated for the current episode on the given agent.
>
> **GetObservations()** – Gets a read-only view of observations generated by the **CollectObservations** method. This method can be useful inside of **Heuristics** to avoid recomputing the observations.

LazyInitialize() – Calls your initialize override if one exists. It can be called multiple times.

OnBeforeSerialize() – Gets called immediately before serialization. Call the base implementation if you're using custom serialization methods.

OnAfterDeserialize() – Gets called immediately after deserialization. Call the base implementation if you're using custom serialization methods.

OnEnable() – This is Unity's **OnEnable** functionality that gets called once the attached **gameobject** becomes **active**. If you implement custom logic, remember to call the base implementation too.

OnDisable() – This is Unity's **OnDisable** functionality that gets called once the attached **gameobject** becomes **inactive**. If you implement custom logic, remember to call the base implementation too.

RequestAction() – Requesting an action repeats the agent's last action from a decision without requesting a new decision.

ScaleAction(float, float, float) – Scales a continuous action from a range of –1:1 to any range you provide.

SetModel(String, NNModel, InferenceDevice) – Sets the model assigned to the agent. You should note that the agent will ignore the behavior name parameter while it is not training. At the same time, it will ignore the model and inference device parameters when not using inference.

That's what makes up an ML-Agent. We'll keep looking deeper into this and eventually build our agent too.

Inputs and Outputs

In inputs and outputs, we will discuss how an ML-Agent can both interpret and interact with the virtual environment around it.

We'll start with the various sensors and observations that our agent can use – our inputs.

Inputs, Observations, and Sensors

The agents we build use a series of float values to visualize the world around them.

However, the word visualize may differ from the first thing that comes to your mind.

You see, an ML-Agent does not "see"; it interprets.

It does this by associating given values and actions with rewards. Perhaps this is why current agents cannot "understand" the tasks we give them. We're still missing some fundamental steps.

The agent is exceptional at finding patterns in data, but our processing power is still limited, so we need to be picky about the data we provide an agent.

The more data, the higher the likelihood of an agent performing well, given the proper reward structure. However, the more data, the slower the training occurs, which means poorer agent performance.

This poorer agent is due to the performance implications and the time taken to reach an ideal state.

So when giving an agent data, we want to find a balance of quantity and relevance.

Suppose we have an agent who aims to launch a ball into a hoop. The agent is entirely blind until we give it observations. So we start to describe its world using observations.

Observations describe the virtual world.

In this example, we may give the agent its position to know where it is in 3D space.

Then we may give the agent the target position of the hoop. These observations will allow the agent to see its position relative to the target.

When constructing an agent, I often like to think about what the agent would see if it were a person, starting with complete nothingness. From there, I add details that have the highest relevancy to the agent's goal.

In this hypothetical example, what does the agent need to know to throw a ball into a hoop?

Let's give it some thought and take a look at Figure 6-6.

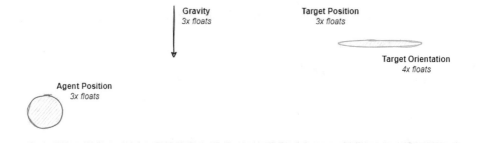

Figure 6-6. *The agent's view of the world in the example*

The agent needs to know two things to throw the ball into the hoop:

- What direction to throw the ball

- How much force is needed

To answer these, we need to understand the distance the ball needs to travel.

To figure that out, we need to understand the agent's position relative to the target and any forces the environment may impart on the ball along the way.

If the target is a hoop, it may also be at an angle, so we might want to know the orientation of the hoop.

So the agent needs to be able to observe

- The agent's position (**Vector3**)

- The target's position (**Vector3**)

- The target's orientation (**Quaternion**)

- Gravity (**Vector3**)

With this information, the agent can attempt a combination of different launch velocities and directions. We then reward the agent whenever the ball enters the hoop.

The whole agent visualization may look something like Figure 6-7.

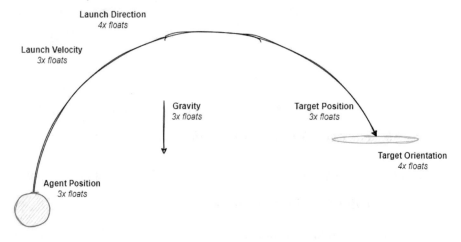

Figure 6-7. *The agent's final view of the world in the example*

We can then optimize this network, reducing the input data until this notably affects our training performance. Suppose the target's position was always relative to the agent; we could eliminate the agent's position observation, which would reduce our observations by three.

Then suppose that we only ever applied gravity in the **Y** axis – we could change gravity from a **Vector3** to a **float** observation, which would reduce our observations by a further two.

Suppose the target orientation was always static – we could remove that observation, eliminating another four observations.

As such, we could go from **13** to **4** observations, considerably simplifying our agent's network and making it more performant for training and inference.

Then we have the action of launching a ball with velocity and direction. We will discuss actions and outputs after this section.

So as you can see, it's essential to describe the world to the agent, using as few observations as possible without sacrificing relevance – again, to strike that balance between as few observations as possible with the most relevance. Figure 6-8 illustrates this point.

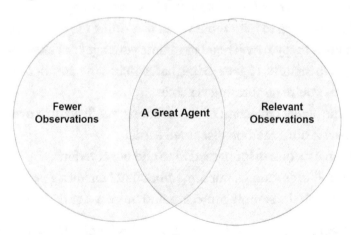

Figure 6-8. *The balance you should aim for when building your agents*

Let's get into discussing the creation of observations.

So How Do We Create Observations?

There are three primary ways for us to generate observations. Let's take a look at these:

- Collecting observations

- Observable attribute

- Implementing the ISensor interface

We'll start by discussing the collection of observations.

Collecting Observations

The first approach, prevalent in Unity ML-Agents, overrides the **CollectOb servations(VectorSensor sensor)** method on the **Agent** class.

We touched on this briefly earlier in this chapter, but I'd like to cover this in more depth, as this is a great way to observe the data of an environment when the data is numerical and nonvisual.

So, the first thing to remember when overriding the collection of observations is that you will need to update your agent's **Behaviour Parameters** to include a **Space Size** that matches the number of vector observations you're performing via code.

To do the actual collection of observations, you'll want to override the CollectObservations method discussed earlier.

You then use the sensor passed in to add observations.

Here is a short example, but remember that I encourage you to tear apart the code in the sample project to find more usage of this:

```
public override void CollectObservations(VectorSensor sensor)
{
    // 3 Observations total, since Vector 3 breaks down into
    // three floats.
    sensor.AddObservation(transform.localPosition);
}
```

If you have a keen eye, you may have noticed that I added the entire local position as an observation, rather than adding each value like the **3DBall** example does. This is because the AddObservation method has many different overloads supporting many of the basic C# and Unity types.

I encourage you to reference the supported types for the AddObservation method discussed earlier in this chapter. It will explain the supported types and how many vector observations they add.

More things to note are that the observations always need to be added in the same order and always be the same quantity of observations during training and inference.

If you ever need to collect a varying number of vector observations, you can do this by padding missing observations with a value of 0.

Another approach is to give yourself a buffer of how many varying observations you plan on making.

Suppose you needed to observe all **gameobjects** in an area around you that represented, say, collectible coins. You could instead look at observing the nearest **ten** coins. If only **four** coins were available, you would pad the rest of the observations with the value of **0**.

Another thing to consider when collecting observations is a unique requirement when creating observations of enums.

Suppose we have the following enum:

```
public enum CreatureDisposition
{
        Aggressive,
        Neutral,
        Passive
}
```

When observing the value of this enum, we need to do so using one-hot encoding, which you can read more about in the following URL:

https://en.wikipedia.org/wiki/One-hot

Failing to use one-hot encoding for categorical information will yield poor results.

Thankfully, ML-Agents provide a fantastic method that removes all of the low-level efforts, allowing us to use the **AddOneHotObservation()** method on our sensor.

To do so, we pass in the currently observed enum cast to an int, followed by the total number of item types in the enum, demonstrated in the following example:

```
public override void CollectObservations(VectorSensor sensor)
{
    // 3 Observations total, since Vector 3 breaks down into
    // three floats.
    sensor.AddOneHotObservation((int)observedEnum,
    totalEnumTypes);
}
```

Remember to update your **observation space** with the total number of enum types on the **behavior parameters** component.

Using the Observable Attribute

The other alternative is the use of observable attributes.

With that said, I would highly avoid using this in performance-critical projects, as the observable attribute uses reflection internally and has worse performance than passing the value through to the collect observations override.

So what are observable attributes?

Observable attributes are field and property attributes that allow the agent to observe the given variable once you've configured the behavior parameters to look for them.

Let's look at the following example:

```
// [Observable(string name = null, int stackedObservations)]
[Observable("Current Health", 3)]
private float currentHealth;
```

The preceding code tells the agent to observe the currentHealth, with a stacked observation count of **3**. The stacked observation allows the agent to store a buffer of **3** observations of current health, allowing it to see the context of the value change.

Thus, the agent can determine if the health is changing and if that change is positive or negative.

Let's break this down further. The observable attribute is the only part that is required.

We can optionally give the observation a name, which is required if this observation is on a sensor, as sensors need unique names.

Additionally, we can optionally specify the number of stacked observations to allow it to view the history of the value by storing it in a buffer.

An important thing to note about the observable attribute is that you do NOT need to increment the observation space in the behavior parameters component. This adjustment is made internally through reflection.

And a final important note is that observables will do nothing by default. You need to enable them in the behavior parameters component by adjusting the ObservableAttributeHandling field to one of the following:

- **Ignore** – The default setting. This setting will ignore all observable attributes of the agent. This option has the best performance as the agent does not use observables or the required reflection.

- **Exclude Inherited** – This setting will only check the class members with the observable attribute. This option is generally the best if you're adamant about using observables.

- **Examine All** – This setting will examine all members of the class. This option has the worst performance and should be avoided, but it is required if your agent inherits from another agent that implements observables.

So overall, the observable attributes are nice for early testing or small projects.

Still, I would personally avoid it and collect the observations through the override instead, purely due to the performance cost of runtime reflection.

So what about the third way?

Creating Sensors

We'll go more in depth into sensors shortly, but the third way of creating observations is by creating a sensor.

You can create a sensor by implementing the **ISensor** interface on your component, like in the following example:

```
public class ExampleSensor : MonoBehaviour, ISensor
```

By implementing the ISensor interface, you are creating what's known as a sensor.

The sensor is responsible for collecting and formatting the data for interpretation by the agent and is interestingly used internally by both **CollectObservations** and **Observables**.

So why bother with **CollectObservations** and **Observables** if sensors are the final destination for observations?

That's because the sensor is intended for advanced users and is mainly abstracted away when it comes to **CollectObservations** and **Observables**.

Sensors are superior to their CollectObservations and Observables counterparts.

While CollectObservations and Observables produce vector observations represented as a list of floats, sensors can do even more.

They can handle vector observations as well as visual observations! The exciting part about this is that visual observations are multidimensional arrays of floats.

So for those brave enough to delve into building a sensor, the next section is for you, despite the extra work that comes with it.

Building Sensors

This next section will discuss how to build your ML-Agent sensor.

This part is more advanced than other parts of this book and will require a solid understanding of programming principles. You are more than welcome to skip this if it's too advanced, as using the **CollectObservations** override is more than sufficient.

Let's begin.

We will build a sensor that observes the nearest entities around the agent up to a maximum observable size.

To find the final example, look in the following directory if you've cloned this book's repository page:

/Assets/Scripts/Sensors/SphereSensor.cs

When implementing the **ISensor** interface, we contract ourselves to implement the following methods:

- **GetObservationSpec()**

- **Write(ObservationWriter writer)**

- **GetCompressedObservation()**

- **Update()**

- **Reset()**

- **GetCompressionSpec()**

- **GetName()**

You must include all these methods in our class and attach a **SensorComponent** to your agent to give the sensor its functionality. The SensorComponent is an abstract class that we will also need to build. Alternatively, you can use a **BasicSensorComponent** for many situations.

We'll discuss each of these methods in detail, starting with **GetObservationSpec**.

GetObservationSpec

GetObservationSpec returns an **ObservationSpec**, which is a struct that describes the details of the given observation. This observation spec tells us things like

- The size of the observation

- The multidimensional properties of the observation

- Observation types that describe whether or not the observation has a goal signal

We can use one of the provided helper methods to create our observation spec based on our requirements.

Three helper methods are available to us:

- **Vector** – This spec describes a one-dimensional observation of the specified length.

- **Visual** – This spec describes a multidimensional observation for visual-like observations containing width, height, and, optionally, multiple channels.

- **VariableLength** – This spec describes observations of variable length.

Vector Observation Spec

The vector observation spec uses the Vector helper method. Let's take a look at the following example:

```
return ObservationSpec.Vector(int length, ObservationType obsType);
```

The preceding helper method takes a length argument, followed by an optional observation type argument. The length argument is the size of the observation.

The observation type defaults to **ObservationType.Default**.

All observation specs have a default observation type. So I will be omitting them from the following examples.

So if one were to observe the current health variable of an enemy, you might do the following:

```
return ObservationSpec.Vector(int 1);
```

The next observation spec helper is the visual method.

Visual Observation Spec

The visual observation spec is ideal for dealing with image-like observations that are multidimensional. The helper method makes describing the complex observation easy. Let's take a look at it:

```
return ObservationSpec.Vector(int height, int width, int channels);
```

This observation spec helper method makes it easy to construct visual observation specs. We need to feed in the height, width, and amount of channels. **Note that height is first, not width.**

Suppose we have a 128x128 RGB render texture that we would like to observe. In this situation, we would use the following code:

```
return ObservationSpec.Vector(int 128, int 128, int 3);
```

However, we won't be using a visual observation spec. Instead, we'll use a variable length sensor for our example sensor, as we don't know how many entities will enter our agent's area. So, we use the **VariableLength** helper method.

Variable Length Observation Spec

The variable length observation spec is ideal when you are unsure how many observations you will have. It allows us to specify the observation size and the maximum number of observations to handle.

```
return ObservationSpec.Vector(int size, int
maximumObservations);
```

So for our use, we want to observe the positions of each entity local to the training environment.

This value will be a Vector3 observation, which results in a size of 3. We will allow the agent to track up to ten observable entities. So, we could write something like the following snippet:

```
return ObservationSpec.Vector(int 3, int 10);
```

That's it. We created our observation spec quickly, thanks to the fantastic helper methods provided by Unity.

The next method to cover is the Write method.

Write

Write allows us to write our observations directly to the **ObservationWriter**. The ObservationWriter is where all the magic happens, and there are many different ways to write to it.

To correctly implement the write method, we need to understand the ObservationWriter better.

ObservationWriter

The **ObservationWriter** allows us to write our observations to the agent. How we do this depends on our data structure. We can largely break this down into the following two groups:

- **Complex types** – **Vector** structs and **Quaternions**
- **Simple types** – Direct **float** observations

We'll start by looking at the simple types.

Writer[index] = observation

Suppose we have one-dimensional observations to make. We can make this observation by directly accessing the writer's buffer. Let's take the following example:

writer[0] = observation;

where the writer is our **ObservationWriter**, 0 is the writer's starting index, and observation is the float value we're looking to write.

You can also do a for-loop and iterate through the writer, but I strongly advise using AddList instead if dealing with lists.

Next, we have the **AddList** method.

AddList(IList<Single>, Int32)

The **AddList** method allows us to add lists of data to the writer. It takes an **IList** of **float** and an **int** offset for the write buffer.

The **AddList** is the part where things get tricky.

If you intend to make multiple calls to **AddList**, for example, if you have multiple lists that you would like to observe, you will need to calculate the appropriate offset.

We can call the following code to add a list of floats to the observation:

```
writer.AddList(observations, 0);
```

Where **0** is the offset, you can omit it if you do not need to change it.

In our situation, we want to add a list of Vector3 observations to our sensor. Let's look at the **Add(Vector3, Int32)** method next.

Add(Vector3, Int32)

The Add helper method for Vectors is straightforward when dealing with a single **Vector3** observation.

However, in our case, we want a list of Vector3 observations. Since **AddList** takes **floats**, we can't use that.

So instead, we will use the Add helper method for **Vector3** and calculate the required offset and padding.

It also becomes more tricky as we support an unknown number of vector observations.

So our first step is to calculate our observation deficit, which asks, "How many observations were missing that we need to pad?"

To calculate our observation deficit, we need to know how large the observation is and how many observations at most to expect.

Since we know that **Vector3**s have an observation size of **3**, we can set this as a constant in our sensor class.

We will then allow the user to specify the maximum number of observations.

We also need a place to store our observations, so we'll create an **Array** of **Vector3**s that we initialize during the Start method.

A reminder that you can find the full code sample for our sensor in the book's repository, under the following directory:

Assets/Scripts/Sensors/SphereSensor.cs

Let's take a look at the following code:

```
const int ObservationSize = 3;

[SerializeField]
private int maximumObservations = 10;

// Initialize this in Start() as an Array of size
maximumObservations.
private IList<Vector3> observations;
```

Now we can use this to calculate our observation deficit, and we can cache our observation count as follows:

```
var observationDeficit = maximumObservations -
observations.Count;
var observationCount = observations.Count;
```

From here, we'll implement the logic for adding our existing observations, as follows:

```
for (int i = 0; i < observationCount; i++)
{
    var offset = i * ObservationSize;
    writer.Add(observations[i], offset);
}
```

The preceding code will write our observations to the writer, but we still need to continue the writing to fill in our padding. So we add a loop that continues where we left off:

```
for (int i = observationCount; i < observationDeficit; i++)
```

117

```
{
    var offset = i * ObservationSize;
    writer.Add(observations[i], offset);
}
```

Then finally, we calculate the total number of observations:

```
return ObservationSize * maximumObservations;
```

That's our implementation of the **Write** method. However, there are a few more to cover. Remember to update your offset accordingly if you intend to add multiple observations, as we did in this example.

Let's discuss **Add(Quaternion, Int32)** next.

Add(Quaternion, Int32)

Much like the vector observation we discussed, this method allows you to record observations. The implementation itself is identical. However, with this one, we can pass in the **Quaternion** type.

Remember that **Quaternion** has an observation size of **4**.

Add(Vector4, Int32)

Again, this method allows you to record observations, as discussed in our Vector3 example. However, with this one, we can pass in **Vector4** observations.

The implementation itself is identical.

Remember that **Vector4** has an observation size of **4**.

That covers the implementation of the Write method in our **ISensor**! Let's move on to the **GetCompressedObservation** method.

GetCompressedObservation

The GetCompressedObservation method allows you to implement custom byte compression. Unity does not recommend using this unless you're working with large visual observations.

To work around this, we can simply **return null**.

Update

The Update method is called during the **UpdateSensors** step internally.

This update happens whenever the agent needs to make a decision. We can use this to run any custom logic on our sensor. We'll be using it to update our observations.

You can find the code in the SphereSensor sample in the directory provided a few pages back.

It's worth noting that during the current release of ML-Agents, version 19, the update method is called every frame due to the Monobehaviour update loop.

It's unclear if this is intentional or if it's a bug. Keep this in mind if working on future versions of ML-Agents. You can follow the opened GitHub issue at the following URL:

https://github.com/Unity-Technologies/ml-agents/issues/5784

Reset

The agent calls Reset whenever its training episode ends. This method typically does not require any implementation and can be left empty.

However, you can add your cleanup implementation here if you need to do any cleanup.

GetCompressionSpec

This method should return information on the compression spec you are using for GetCompressedObservation.

In almost all cases, you won't end up using this as it's only used internally by the camera sensor for custom compression to PNG, which anyway results in poor performance.

You can simply return **CompressionSpec.Default**.

Let's move on to the next method, **GetName**.

GetName

This method should return the unique name of the sensor. In most cases, I suggest setting up a constant in the class containing the name and returning that value.

If you intend to have multiple of the same type of sensor on a given agent, then you should expose this name field, and each sensor should have a unique name.

Visual Observations

There are a few ways to work with visual observations. These are

- A custom **ISensor** implementation

- **CameraSensor** component

- **RenderTextureSensor** component

These various sensors collect observations of the image data and transform that data into a multidimensional tensor.

In essence, a tensor is an algebraic object which describes the multilinear relationship between groups of other algebraic objects within a vector space. We use tensors extensively in machine learning.

We then feed this tensor into a convolutional neural network or CNN.

Doing this allows the agent to learn from the spatial patterns and regularities within the visual observations.

You are also not limited to using either a vector or visual observations. An agent is capable of using both.

Visual observations are ideal for situations where it may be difficult to describe the environment numerically via vector observations. However, visual observations have far worse performance and training time than vector observations.

So, while visual observations benefit specific niche applications, you should only use them as a last resort or if a visual observation would satisfy your requirements.

Alternatively, you can use visual observations in conjunction with vector observations.

This hybrid approach is often superior as an agent trained purely on visual observations will often be worse at performing a given task than an agent trained on the appropriate vector observations.

Visual observations offer some unique benefits, especially when building ML-Agent-enabled robotics, as you can feed a physical camera's data into a render texture that the agent can observe.

Visual observations also support stacking, which can be useful in many situations but negatively impacts performance, so you should only use it as necessary.

Out of the box, you can give your agent visual observations by attaching a **CameraSensor** or a **RenderTextureSensor** to your agent.

The alternative is to create a custom **ISensor** that handles visual observations, but this is outside this book's scope as **CameraSensor** and **RenderTextureSensor** are sufficient for most cases.

You should also keep the image size as small as possible without losing the required visual fidelity to complete the task. By keeping the image size small, you'll mitigate more of the performance impact of visual observations.

If color information is irrelevant to completing the task, you should use grayscale images, significantly improving training time.

Many other sensors are available with the ML-Agents extensions we installed during our setup chapter. Let's take a look at these.

The ML-Agents extensions package contains various experimental features and sensors.

The sensors cater to physics interactions and joints. The most notable addition in ML-Agents extensions is the ability to create custom grid sensors if you'd like to apply the knowledge you learned in the "Building Sensors" section of this chapter and apply it.

Since the extensions are highly experimental and subject to change, we won't be covering them, but they are still worth a mention if you are curious enough.

Let's move on to discussing actions.

Actions

Actions are instructions from the agent Policy – the brain – for the agent to perform.

We interpret the action through an **ActionBuffer**, which the agent can use to receive actions.

Alternatively, you can implement a custom **IActuator** to handle the actions.

ML-Agents has the concept of two types of actions:

- **Continuous**

- **Discrete**

An important thing to understand about ML-Agents is that they do not understand their actions. The system simply tries different combinations of actions based on the inputs and the correlated reward.

We use the **OnActionReceived()** override on the Agent class to access and implement functionality to the ML-Agent's actions.

To specify the number of actions and discrete branches the agent should support, we can modify the respective fields in the **BehaviourParameters** field. Adjusting this value will allow us to access these actions in the **OnActionReceived** override on the agent.

We discussed this override briefly earlier when we discussed the Agent class. It's time for us to look at this override in more detail, but, first, we need to understand the difference between **Continuous** and **Discrete** actions.

Continuous

When the **BehaviourParameters** have continuous actions specified, the agent will attempt to use them, passing the output values to the OnActionReceived override on the agent.

To utilize continuous actions, we override the OnActionReceived method of our agent and access the **ActionBuffer** with an array accessor. As best practice, we should clamp the value from the **ActionBuffer** to a range of **-1 : 1**.

We can then add our logic that utilizes the action's value. Let's take a look at the following code example:

```
public override void OnActionReceived(ActionBuffers
actionBuffers)
{
    var myAction1 = Mathf.Clamp(actionBuffers.
    ContinuousActions[0], -1f, 1f);
    var myAction2 = Mathf.Clamp(actionBuffers.
    ContinuousActions[1], -1f, 1f);
    ar myAction3 = Mathf.Clamp(actionBuffers.
    ContinuousActions[2], -1f, 1f);
    DoLogicWithAction1(myAction1);
    DoLogicWithAction1(myAction2);
    DoLogicWithAction1(myAction3);
}
```

It's important to remember that the values received have no inherent meaning to the agent because the agent doesn't understand what it's doing. These values become usable based on the action-reward cycle that happens during training. The agent just learns that some value for action buffer at index 0 is good when it receives a specific observation because of the reward we give it.

The same concept applies to discrete actions.

Discrete

Discrete actions work using the concept of branches. Firstly, in the **BehaviourParameters** component, we specify the number of branches, after which we specify how many outcomes each of those branches should support.

The agent then passes us an ActionBuffer containing each of the branches.

The action buffer branch then contains a selection of which end node the agent selected.

This choice is represented to us in an integer index, with a range of **0:BranchSize**.

Let's examine the following example:

```
// 2 Discrete Actions specified within the BehaviourParameters.
// Choice 1 contains a branch size of 2. If the value is 0, do
// nothing. If the value is 1, do something specific to
choice 1.
var choice1 = actionBuffers.DiscreteActions[0];
// Choice 2 contains a branch size of 2. If the value is 0, do
//nothing. If the value is 1, do something specific to
choice 2.
var choice2 = actionBuffers.DiscreteActions[1];
switch (choice1)
{
    case 0:
        DoNothing();
        break;
    case 1:
        DoSomethingSpecificToTreeOne();
        break;
}
```

```
switch (choice2)
{
    case 0:
        DoNothing();
        break;
    case 1:
        DoSomethingSpecificToTreeTwo();
        break;
}
```

The benefit of discrete actions is the ability to mask actions. By masking actions, we can prevent a specific action from happening if a different discrete action is satisfied.

We do this by overriding the WriteDiscreteActionMask method on the agent. We then specify the branch we're writing the mask to and pass in the index of the action, followed by if we want to allow the action.

After each step, the agent resets all masks, allowing all actions.

Let's look at the following example:

```
public override void WriteDiscreteActionMask
(IDiscreteActionMask actionMask)
{
    actionMask.SetActionEnabled(branch, actionIndex,
    isAllowed);
}
```

Continuous actions do not support action masking; if you want the ability to mask actions, you should leverage discrete actions for those situations.

It's important to note that you cannot write a discrete action mask to a continuous action. Another important note is that when using heuristics, discrete action masks are ignored!

So what are heuristics?

Heuristics

Heuristics allow us to gain manual control over an agent's actions. They're beneficial for debugging and imitation learning.

We need to override the Heuristic method on the agent to use heuristics:

```
public override void Heuristic(float[] actionsOut)
{
    // manualValue can be any value we want as a float.
    actionsOut[0] = manualValue;
}
```

Heuristics are used to override the agent's actions, allowing us to make decisions manually on behalf of the agent. We typically do this by binding actions to Unity's Input System.

It's important to note that imitation learning requires a heuristics override.

Now that we know about inputs, generating actions, and requesting decisions, we should look at rewards.

Rewards

Earlier in the book, we discussed how reinforcement learning utilizes reward values to train the agent. Next, we'll discuss how to implement those rewards.

We do this by calling AddReward and SetReward on our agent. We touched on these methods earlier in the chapter, but as a quick refresher:

- **AddReward** – Increments the agent's reward for the current episode. This method is much like the pseudo expression: **reward += value;**

- **SetReward** – Sets the agent's reward for the current episode. This method is much like the pseudo expression: `reward = value;`

Let's discuss the SetReward method in more detail first. SetReward is ideal for penalizing critical mistakes; you should use it sparingly.

Suppose the agent collides with an enemy, a critical mistake in our situation. We can implement something like the following code on our agent:

```
private void OnCollisionEnter(Collision collision)
{
    // If the agent touches an enemy, add a negative reward
    and end the
  // episode.
    if (collision.gameObject.CompareTag("enemy"))
    {
        SetReward(-1.0f);
        EndEpisode();
    }
}
```

In the preceding situation, absolutely anything the agent does is irrelevant if the agent collides with an enemy collider. We penalize the agent and end the episode, which disallows the agent any more opportunity to be rewarded again for that episode.

This approach can be helpful in some situations but will often result in the agent missing out on crucial learning opportunities.

In almost all situations, I would instead encourage the use of AddReward.

AddReward and SetReward can also be called externally by reference to the agent as the methods are public.

Let's take a look at our preferred approach, **AddReward**.

With AddReward, we slightly reward our agents based on if they've done something beneficial to their goal or penalize them if they haven't.

It's crucial not to overpenalize your agent, as this can adversely affect training. You should also try to keep your **AddReward** values normalized to a range of **-1:1** to improve training stability.

Another excellent tip for time-sensitive tasks is to add a minor penalty for every step in which the agent did not achieve the goal. Something along the lines of **-0.01:-0.05** is ideal for many situations.

Let's take a look at the following code example:

```
private void OnCollisionEnter(Collision collision)
{
    if (collision.gameObject.CompareTag("objective"))
    {
        AddReward(0.5f);
    }
}

public override void OnActionReceived(ActionBuffers
actionBuffers)
{

    . . . . . .
        AddReward(-0.03f);
}
```

We reward the player positively for reaching its goal, but we penalize it for each step to discourage it from taking too long to achieve the goal; the overall result is that the agent attempts to do the job quicker to get a higher reward.

This approach encourages the agent to seek out and touch objectives as fast as possible to maximize its final score at the end of each episode.

Keeping the rewards in clamped ranges gives us a more stable training experience.

Finally, we now understand everything required to train an agent. It's time for us to learn to train an agent.

Training an Agent

Before we jump into creating and training our own agent, we'll learn how to train an existing agent so that you can experience the training process with as few issues as possible.

We're going to be retraining the 3DBall sample.

1) The first step is to open the 3DBall sample scene. If you cloned the example repository during the setup chapter, then you will be able to find it in the following location:

Assets/ML-Agents/3DBall/Scenes/3DBall.unity

2) As an additional step, go to

Edit ➤ Project Settings ➤ Player ➤ Resolution and Presentation ➤ Enable the "Run in Background" checkbox.

The training process uses the Python **mlagents** package we installed during the setup chapter.

The success of training an ML-Agent is also largely influenced by hyperparameters.

We glanced over hyperparameters earlier in the book, and we'll skip past them for now. For now, know that you can find some example hyperparameter configurations in the following directory if you've cloned the example repository for the book:

Assets/ML-Agents/config

For training the 3DBall sample, we will be using the hyperparameters that Unity provided for their 3DBall sample. You can find this under ../**Assets/ML-Agents/config/ppo/3DBall.yaml**.

3) Open and activate your Python virtual environment as you did in the setup chapter.

From here, you want to run the following command:

`mlagents-learn [3DBall.yaml file full path] --run-id=3DBall-Example-1`

You can break the command down into the following:

- mlagents-learn – This command tells Python that you want to use ML-Agents.

- [3DBall.yaml file full path] – Here, you should insert the full path to the hyperparameter YAML file. This argument should include the file name and extension and exclude the square brackets.

- –run-id=3DBall-Example-1 – This argument is required to specify a unique name for the training profile. This argument will store your results in a directory name of your choosing and allow you to resume past training sessions.

  Optionally, you can pass in the **--resume** argument if you wish to resume training of the given id or **--force** if you wish to overwrite the training. **One of these is required if a training session with the given run-id already exists!**

  This command should display the Unity logo in the terminal, and shortly afterward it will display the following message:

[INFO] Listening on port 5004. Start training by pressing the Play button in the Unity Editor.

4)   Once you receive that message, you're ready to begin training. Click the Play button in Unity to begin training!

The training will then commence, and you will start to receive training update messages roughly every 15 seconds. The messages look something like the following:

[INFO] 3DBall. Step: 36000. Time Elapsed: 15.162 s. Mean Reward: 1.953. Std of Reward: 1.551. Training.

We're interested in seeing the mean reward value increase over time as the agent trains. If the mean reward increases over time, it's a good indicator that the agent is improving.

You may notice that the mean reward very gradually improves or even worsens near the start of the training. Then, once the agent starts to improve, it undergoes rapid improvement. This slow start, followed by a learning explosion, is a typical pattern when training ML-Agents.

Your console should look something like this:

[INFO] 3DBall. Step: 36000. Time Elapsed: 15.162 s. Mean Reward: 1.953. Std of Reward: 1.551. Training. [INFO] 3DBall. Step: 48000. Time Elapsed: 40.273 s. Mean Reward: 2.312. Std of Reward: 1.741. Training. [INFO] 3DBall. Step: 60000. Time Elapsed: 59.462 s. Mean Reward: 3.517. Std of Reward: 2.722. Training. [INFO] 3DBall. Step: 72000. Time Elapsed: 79.986 s. Mean Reward: 6.551. Std of Reward: 6.456. Training. [INFO] 3DBall. Step: 84000. Time Elapsed: 98.850 s. Mean Reward: 24.485. Std of Reward: 23.905. Training.

```
[INFO] 3DBall. Step: 96000. Time Elapsed: 118.766 s.
Mean Reward: 50.343. Std of Reward: 36.911. Training.
[INFO] 3DBall. Step: 108000. Time Elapsed: 135.078 s.
Mean Reward: 83.564. Std of Reward: 27.168. Training.
[INFO] 3DBall. Step: 120000. Time Elapsed: 153.034 s.
Mean Reward: 93.646. Std of Reward: 17.563. Training.
[INFO] 3DBall. Step: 132000. Time Elapsed: 170.700 s.
Mean Reward: 92.631. Std of Reward: 17.688. Training.
[INFO] 3DBall. Step: 144000. Time Elapsed: 188.461 s.
Mean Reward: 100.000. Std of Reward: 0.000. Training.
[INFO] 3DBall. Step: 156000. Time Elapsed: 206.732 s.
Mean Reward: 97.742. Std of Reward: 7.490. Training.
[INFO] 3DBall. Step: 168000. Time Elapsed: 219.169 s.
Mean Reward: 100.000. Std of Reward: 0.000. Training.
[INFO] 3DBall. Step: 180000. Time Elapsed: 237.326 s.
Mean Reward: 100.000. Std of Reward: 0.000. Training.
```

5) Once your mean reward reaches a value that you're
    satisfied with or reaches the ceiling at which it can
    no longer improve, select the console and press
    Control + **C** to stop the training cycle.

    The training will stop, and ML-Agents will export the
    current model.

```
[INFO] Learning was interrupted. Please wait while the
graph is generated.
[INFO] Exported results\3DBall-
Example-1\3DBall\3DBall-324455.onnx
[INFO] Copied results\3DBall-
Example-1\3DBall\3DBall-324455.onnx to results\3DBall-
Example-1\3DBall.onnx.
```

6) Once you receive these messages indicating that the export is complete, ensure that your Unity is no longer in play mode.

7) From there, head to your Virtual Environment folder and follow the directory that ML-Agents provided.

In my case:

..\Virtual Environment\results\3DBall-Example-1\3DBall.onnx

From here, copy this file into your Unity assets folder. **If you are experiencing issues copying the file by dragging it into the Unity "Project" tab, consider using file explorer instead.** Congratulations, you've just trained your first agent. The next step is to assign this model to our agents.

8) To do this, search for Agent in your hierarchy.

9) Then select all agents using Shift + left click.

10) Finally, drag the model from your assets folder into the Model field on your agents.

You are telling the agents to use your model file for inference by assigning your model.

To test it out, click the play button. If you've trained your agents to a mean reward of roughly 100 for this sample, then the agents will be good enough at the task to almost never fail.

You can refer to Figure 6-9 if you are stuck.

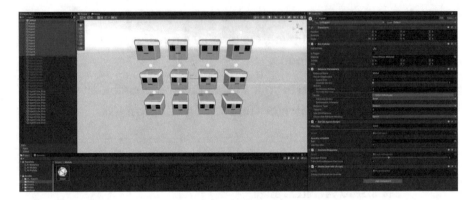

Figure 6-9. *The model assignment process*

Well done on making it this far! Let's wrap up this chapter before moving on to building our very first agent.

Conclusion

It's been a long and information-packed chapter. Let's recap what we learned.

This chapter taught us about the agent, its various overrides, and public methods.

We covered how to grant rewards or penalties to your agents. We learned how to do this in a way that results in a more stable learning curve for the agent.

We covered the various forms of inputs and outputs and how this translates into an agent interacting with the world.

We covered building a custom sensor for advanced users from the ground up. We discussed the various types of observations and discussed visual observations.

Then we learned about heuristics, and we trained our own agent!

In the next chapter, we'll build our own agent, train it, and run it from the ground up.

There were many useful tips and tricks in this chapter, but here are a few to remember:

- Keep your rewards small, within the range of -1:1, to ensure a smooth, stable training experience for your agents.

- Don't overuse negative penalties, or your agent may not learn any meaningful actions from the training process.

- Keep your visual observations as small as possible and only use them when describing an environment with numeric values is very difficult.

- Experiment with the samples provided!

- Keep your observations relevant; useless observations will only lead to slower training times and runtime performance loss.

Let's begin building our own agent in the next chapter!

CHAPTER 7

Creating Your First AI in Unity

Now that you know the basics, it's time to use that knowledge. In this chapter, I'll guide you in creating your first ML-Agent from scratch.

We'll go through the planning necessary, explore potential reward schemes, discuss how we will have our agent perceive the world around it, and discuss the various challenges we may face.

We'll then put this to the test and build your first ML-Agent. We'll develop and prepare the environment and the challenge that the agent will face.

Then you'll learn about hyperparameters and how they can drastically affect training time and performance.

We'll wrap up by training your new ML-Agent and discuss various techniques to speed up the training, from multiple training zones to concurrent runtimes connected to the same PyTorch instance.

I will show you how to use TensorBoard and highlight how important it is in the ML-Agent workflow.

Finally, we'll polish the ML-Agent, deploy the model, and watch our new creation. I hope you learn a lot from this chapter and have fun while learning.

© Dylan Engelbrecht 2023
D. Engelbrecht, *Introduction to Unity ML-Agents*,
https://doi.org/10.1007/978-1-4842-8998-3_7

Planning an Agent

Sharpening the proverbial axe is an essential aspect of developing ML-Agents.

Reinforcement learning can be unpredictable if you are unprepared. So to develop a great agent, we need to plan. In this section, we'll do just that.

You are welcome to follow my example, as the example will be available on the GitHub repository, but I encourage you to take a swing at your own design, following the principles you learn here even if you come back later after following the example.

ML-Agent development takes experience; the best way to get experience is to throw yourself at it and try your best. With that said, start small and keep it simple, stupid – KISS.

Let's discuss the example that I'll be putting together.

The Avoidance Sample

The avoidance sample will aim to train an agent capable of dodging and evading objects moving at variable speeds around its environment.

For this, we will need an agent capable of moving along the world X and Z coordinates and objects for the agent to avoid.

The agent should be able to move at variable speeds, up to a maximum speed, in any combination of the XZ axis.

We will also create several smaller objects that move freely around the training zone for the challenge – starting in a random direction and speed and bouncing off the boundaries of the training area and each other.

The avoidable objects will utilize object pooling to help with performance and respawn whenever the agent fails by touching them.

They should also avoid spawning directly on top of the agent.

The agent's goal will be to stay alive for as long as possible, avoiding these avoidable objects.

Let's look at Figure 7-1.

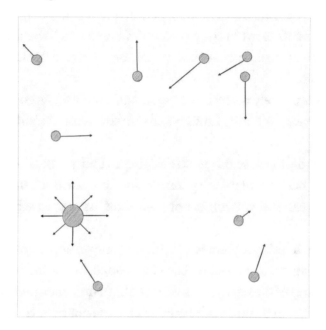

Figure 7-1. *The avoidables sample concept*

The next step is to plan how we will reward the agent for achieving our desired goal, so let's do that next.

Reward Scheme

Planning a good reward scheme for an agent is vital to the success of your training pipeline. This part can often be one of the most challenging steps to get right.

For example, I had planned on rewarding the agent for every step that did not collide with avoidables in the avoidables sample. While, in theory, this is a solid approach for agents that need to survive as long as they can, in practice, it's a bit different.

An earlier version of the avoidables sample had a flaw.

Agents discovered that the likelihood of being hit by avoidables was dramatically lower in the corners of the training environment. So they would find the best available corner and hug it, performing minor movements to avoid stray avoidables moving into their sacred little corners – or in rare cases, they abandoned their corner in favor of another corner.

And this is entirely correct – the agent had achieved its goal perfectly. However, this was not quite how I wanted to showcase the ability of ML-Agents.

I wanted to showcase the agent dodging as many avoidables as possible. So I had to amend the planning for the reward scheme.

So as you can see, you might not always get the reward scheme right the first time.

A solution to this problem is a technique known as reward shaping, sometimes referred to as reward-based guidance. In reward-based guidance, you give the agent rewards for completing intermediary steps. However, it's worth noting that reward shaping is not perfect, and it's important to learn how to do it right. That's why I'm going to show you how to implement it.

The most common issue with reward shaping is that an agent can end up prioritizing the reward shaping over the primary reward.

In most scenarios, you want to avoid this in favor of curriculum learning, which I will show you in the next chapter.

However, in this scenario, we were fortunate to have a case where **minor** reward-based guidance would benefit the agent. So I modified the agent to get a minor reward with a fall-off value based on its distance to the center of the training environment.

This reward took some tweaking, as the agent initially decided that the death penalty was a bargain price for getting that additional reward at the center of the environment.

So I tweaked this reward so low that early training would almost not even notice the reward.

Suppose your agent struggles to achieve the end goal and focuses too much on the reward generated by reward shaping. In that case, you should consider reducing the intermediary reward or consider curriculum learning.

A key indicator that this is happening is that your agent will abuse the intermediary reward, resulting in an agent that never achieves the desired end goal while still achieving a high reward score.

So, always plan your reward scheme – try and foresee issues in advance, even if you don't always get it right.

To do this, ask what the end goal should be.

For the avoidables agent, we want our end goal to be that the agent survives for as long as possible – and does it in style. So our final reward scheme looks like this:

- Passively earn a small reward for every step alive as the primary goal is to stay alive for as long as possible.

- Passively earn a tiny fraction of a reward based on the distance to the center of the training environment, as the secondary goal is to achieve the primary goal in style.

This reward setup should encourage the agent to favor the center of the map but still place the most priority on staying alive as its primary objective.

The next step in our planning phase is to decide how our agent will observe the virtual world around it. Let's dig into this next.

Observation Plans

The next thing we need to plan is our agent's observation of the virtual world. I want to take an approach that will give you the most experience with various sensors and show you that it's possible to stack custom sensors.

So for the avoidables sample, I'd like to use the following two custom sensors:

- A ray perception sensor, with a custom rotational lock, will allow our agent to determine the direction and distance to avoidables. We can stack these observations to allow the agent to infer velocity and direction.

- A grid sensor with a moderately high resolution and stacked observations will allow our agent to have additional supporting information about the avoidables near it. This sensor will be especially useful if there is an avoidable behind another avoidable.

So while vector observations would work for this situation, I want to expose you to the preceding sensors that can handle varying observables.

The **RayPerceptionSensor** and the **GridSensor** are both included in the ML-Agents package and are excellent for various use cases.

The next part to discuss is how our agent will interact with the world.

Actions Planning

For our actions, we want something that gives the agent greater control over itself in the movement space. To do this, I will encourage continuous actions, allowing the agent to control its speed and direction.

Discrete actions typically train faster, but that doesn't necessarily mean it's better for every use case.

For the avoidables sample, I want the agent to have the ability to swerve and weave itself through avoidables. To do that, we need a range of values between **-1:1** on our actions; continuous actions are ideal here.

So the action space will be pretty straightforward. We need an action for controlling the horizontal input and another for controlling the vertical input – from a top-down perspective.

This setup brings our action space to **2** while allowing the agent to move diagonally at any angle using a combination of actions.

Let's discuss the challenges that we should expect next.

Expected Challenges

While you can't always anticipate every challenge – for example, the agent hiding in corners without incentive to stay near the center – you should always try your best to expect the unexpected.

For the avoidables sample, we have the following expected challenges:

- Balancing our reward structure to ensure that the agent prioritizes staying alive over everything else

- Ensuring that the agent learns anything meaningful while failing

- Validating that we configure our reward scheme and hyperparameters well enough to facilitate the development of an efficient and effective agent

Learning to anticipate challenges comes mostly from practice and experience – so remember to throw yourself into ML challenges frequently. The best way to do this is to build more ML-Agents, leading me to our next topic.

Building Your First ML-Agent

Now that we've done some planning, it's time to start building your first agent.

For this, the code is available on the GitHub repository, as I'm sure you'd rather read code in your IDE than directly from the book. I'll discuss the general idea of the code here.

You can find the code in the following directories:

\Assets\Scripts\Avoidables
\Assets\Scripts\Utility
\Assets\Scripts\Spawners

First, we need to create a controller for our agent. This controller will be a class that inherits from **Agent**. Our first goal is to get this agent controller working with heuristic controls.

By getting the heuristic controls working, we can debug and test to ensure that the core movement functionality of our agent is working.

1) Create a class called **AvoidablesAgent**, which will inherit from the **Agent** class.

   I want the avoidables sample to use a Rigidbody-based movement system, where we dynamically apply force to the agent to get it rolling around the environment.

2) For this, create a variable to control our agent's max speed and acceleration to get movement working.

   ```
   [SerializeField]
   private float maxSpeed = 5f;    ⚡ '3'
   [SerializeField]
   private float acceleration = 3f;    ⚡ Unchanged
   [SerializeField]
   private Rigidbody rb;    ⚡ Changed in 2 assets
   ```

   Once we have that, we can start setting up our actions.

3) We know that we want two continuous actions from our planning: one for movement in the X axis and one for movement in the Y axis. You can access the continuous actions through the ActionBuffers of the OnActionReceived override.

For best practice, we need to clamp the values we receive to the –1:1 range. Let's look at the following code:

```
public override void OnActionReceived(ActionBuffers actionBuffer)
{
    var inputX:float = Mathf.Clamp(value:actionBuffer.ContinuousActions[0], min:-1f, max:1f);
    var inputZ:float = Mathf.Clamp(value:actionBuffer.ContinuousActions[1], min:-1f, max:1f);

    rb.AddForce(x:inputX * acceleration, y:0f, z:inputZ * acceleration, ForceMode.Force);
}
```

Then we can proceed to use these actions to drive our Rigidbody forces. I'll use the **AddForce()** method on our attached **Rigidbody**.

In the **AddForce()** method, I'll use our inputs multiplied by our acceleration to create a new direction for our agent.

4) To clamp our agent to the maximum speed, we'll use Unity's **FixedUpdate()** method to clamp the magnitude of our agent's velocity to our max speed, which can be seen in the following code snippet:

```
private void FixedUpdate()
{
    rb.velocity = Vector3.ClampMagnitude(rb.velocity, maxSpeed);
    var thisTransform = transform;
    var position:Vector3 = thisTransform.localPosition;
    position.y = 0.25f;
    thisTransform.localPosition = position;
}
```

5) The next step is to feed our debugging data to the
    ActionBuffers using the **Heuristic()** override.

    To do this, we must cache the **ContinuousActions** from the
    ActionBuffers inside the **Heuristic()** override. Once cached,
    we can use an array accessor to access and modify the data.

```
public override void Heuristic(in ActionBuffers actionsOut)
{
    var continuousActionsOut :ActionSegment<float>  = actionsOut.ContinuousActions;

    // Increase horizontal velocity.
    continuousActionsOut[0] = Input.GetAxis("Horizontal");
    // Increase vertical velocity.
    continuousActionsOut[1] = Input.GetAxis("Vertical");
}
```

For the override data, we'll be using **Input.
GetAxis("Horizontal")** and **Input.GetAxis("Vertical")**.
There are better ways to implement this input using Unity's new
Input System, but this will suffice as we're only going to be using
the **Heuristic** override in-editor for the avoidables sample.

6) We then need to feed this input to the cached
    continuous actions via an array accessor. This data
    will now override the agent's decisions if it's using
    heuristics.

7) An extra thing that we want to do is to clamp
    the agent's local Y position to prevent it from
    bouncing into the air when colliding with
    surfaces at high speed. We can do this during the
    FixedUpdate() step.

```
private void FixedUpdate()
{
    rb.velocity = Vector3.ClampMagnitude(rb.velocity, maxSpeed);
    var thisTransform = transform;
    var position:Vector3 = thisTransform.localPosition;
    position.y = 0.25f;
    thisTransform.localPosition = position;
}
```

When working with ML-Agents, try to get into the habit of working in local space, especially with observations, as world-space observations may impair the agent.

8) Your agent should now be capable of movement. To test this out, create a parent gameobject for our training zone, and add an environment.

   If you are following along from the cloned sample for this book, then you can find a copy of the barebones environment in the following directory:

   \Assets\Scenes\Avoidance\Prefabs\Training Area - No Logic.prefab

9) The next step is to create an object for our agent. I'll be using a sphere for the agent to facilitate its ability to roll.

10) Attach your agent controller and a **DecisionRequester** component. Your agent **MUST** request decisions for heuristics to work.

11) Finally, ensure that your agent's behavior parameters have a **Continuous Actions** space of 2.

12) Click the play button and use WASD or the arrow keys to move your agent around.

If your agent does not move, remember to assign it an acceleration and max speed value above zero, and ensure that the agent has a Rigidbody. Also, ensure that your agent component has a reference to the Rigidbody.

If you set up everything correctly, your agent should now move when you are in play mode and give it inputs.

13) Our next step is to allow the agent to respawn. We'll use the overrides Initialize() and OnEpisodeBegin() for this.

```
public override void Initialize()
{
    var spawnPosition:Vector3 = Random.insideUnitSphere * spawnRadiusWhenReset;
    var thisTransform = transform;
    spawnPosition.y = thisTransform.parent.position.y + thisTransform.localScale.y / 2f;
    thisTransform.localPosition = spawnPosition;
    var maxReward:float = MaxStep * (rewardPerStep + centerDistanceReward);
    Debug.Log(message:"Agent initialization complete. Theoretical max reward:" + maxReward);
}
```

Try to work in **local space** so the environment can be copy-pasted several times around the scene in a later step.

For the spawning, I'll use a simple **Random.insideUnitSphere** multiplied with a variable for the spawn radius when reset. I'll also expose a UnityEvent that will allow us to notify the environment whenever the agent resets.

14) Great! Next, we'll create the avoidables that the agent must avoid, along with a spawner.

For this, we want another smaller sphere with a Rigidbody. We'll create a controller that allows it to move in a random direction with its local Y clamped. I'll also add functionality to allow it to reflect its velocity on collisions.

14.1) The avoidable obstacle controller should have a speed variable and a reference to its Rigidbody component. I will also create a Vector3 cached variable that we will use shortly.

```
[SerializeField]
private float speed = 2f;  ✦ "0.3"

[SerializeField]
private Rigidbody rb;  ✦ Changed in 1 asset

private Vector3 direction;
```

14.2)   Add the logic for keeping the ball in motion.
For this, I'll have the obstacle pick a random
direction on the XY axis and move in that
direction.

```
private void OnEnable()
{
    direction = new Vector3(x:Random.Range(-1f, 1f), y:0f, z:Random.Range(-1f, 1f));
    rb.velocity = direction * speed;
}

↻ Event function  ◇    ⚲ Dylan "VoidFletcher" Engelbrecht
private void FixedUpdate()
{
    rb.velocity = direction * speed;
}
```

14.3)   Finally, let's allow our avoidable obstacle to
reflect its velocity based on collision.

```
private void OnCollisionEnter(Collision collision)
{
    direction = Vector3.Reflect(direction, collision.contacts[0].normal);
    direction.y = 0;

    rb.velocity = direction * speed;
}
```

15) Next, we need a spawner to create these avoidable obstacles in our training environment.

15.1) Give your spawner the following variables:

```
[SerializeField]
private GameObject avoidablePrefab;      ⚘ Avoidable
[SerializeField]
private Transform avoidablesPoolParent;    ⚘ Changed in 2 assets
[SerializeField]
private LayerMask avoidableLayerMask;    ⚘ Serializable
[SerializeField]
private int maxAvoidables = 10;    ⚘ Changed in 2 assets
[SerializeField]
private float spawnRadius = 10f;    ⚘ "4.33"


        private GameObject[] avoidablesPool;
        private int avoidablesPoolIndex = 0;
        private float spawnDelay = 0.1f;
        private float spawnTimer = 0f;
        private bool isSpawning = true;
        private int activeAvoidables = 0;
```

15.2) Expose a public method that resets the spawned avoidables. We will use this later to reset all of the avoidable obstacles when your agent fails.

```
public void ResetSpawning()
{
    for (int i = 0; i < maxAvoidables; i++)
    {
        avoidablesPool[i].SetActive(false);
    }

    activeAvoidables = 0;
    avoidablesPoolIndex = 0;
}
```

15.3) For performance, I'd encourage the use of a
basic pooling system on your spawner.

```
private void Start ()
{
    avoidablesPool = new GameObject[maxAvoidables];
    for (int i = 0; i < maxAvoidables; i++)
    {
        avoidablesPool[i] = Instantiate(avoidablePrefab, avoidablesPoolParent);
        avoidablesPool[i].SetActive(false);
    }
}
```

15.4) During the update cycle, check if we can
spawn, and if we can, then spawn new
avoidable obstacles.

```
private void Update ()
{
    if (!isSpawning)
    {
        return;
    }

    spawnTimer += Time.deltaTime;
    if (spawnTimer >= spawnDelay && activeAvoidables < maxAvoidables)
    {
        spawnTimer = 0f;
        Spawn();
    }
}
```

15.5) Create a spawning method to handle the
spawning of your avoidables.

```
private void Spawn()
{
    var validSpawnLocationFound = false;
    var maxAttempts = 10;
    while (!validSpawnLocationFound)
    {
        Vector3 spawnPosition = Random.insideUnitSphere * spawnRadius;
        spawnPosition.y = transform.position.y + avoidablePrefab.transform.localScale.y / 2f;
        spawnPosition = transform.TransformPoint(spawnPosition);
        RaycastHit hit;
        var raycastOrigin:Vector3 = spawnPosition + (Vector3.up * 2f);
        raycastOrigin = avoidablesPoolParent.TransformPoint(raycastOrigin);

        var obstructionRadius = 10f;
        if (Physics.SphereCast(
                raycastOrigin,
                obstructionRadius ,
                direction:Vector3.down,
                out hit,
                maxDistance:4f,
                (int)avoidableLayerMask))
        {
            maxAttempts--;


                if (maxAttempts <= 0)
                {
                    break;
                }

                continue;
        }

        avoidablesPool[avoidablesPoolIndex].transform.position = spawnPosition;
        avoidablesPool[avoidablesPoolIndex].SetActive(true);
        avoidablesPoolIndex++;
        activeAvoidables++;
        if (avoidablesPoolIndex >= maxAvoidables)
        {
            avoidablesPoolIndex = 0;
        }

        validSpawnLocationFound = true;
    }
}
```

16) Finally, on the agent, if the agent collides with any AvoidableObstacleController, then go ahead and fail the agent by rewarding it with a value of –1f, and for extra measure, reset the agent's position.

   You should also expose and invoke a UnityEvent that we can use to notify the spawner that the agent failed.

```
private void OnCollisionEnter(Collision collision)
{
    if (collision.gameObject.GetComponent<AvoidableObstacleController>())
    {
        FailAgent();
    }
}
```

   The FailAgent method is detailed on the next page.

```
private void FailAgent()
{
    AddReward(increment: -1f);
    onEpisodeBeginEvent?.Invoke();
    var spawnPosition:Vector3 = Random.insideUnitSphere * spawnRadiusWhenReset;
    var thisTransform = transform;
    var parent:Transform = thisTransform.parent;
    spawnPosition.y = parent.position.y + thisTransform.localScale.y / 2f;
    rb.position = parent.TransformPoint(spawnPosition);
    rb.velocity = Vector3.zero;
}
```

17) Hook your agent's exposed UnityEvent to the **ResetSpawning()** method on your avoidable obstacle controller.

   It might be tempting to end the episode whenever the agent fails, and while this can work in some cases, in this case, it may work against us, as the agent may fail to learn anything meaningful from its failures.

18) Go ahead and test that the foundation of your code works using heuristics.

Once you're happy with the scene, we can move on to giving our agent observations and adding positive rewards.

19) We'll start by adding positive rewards.

19.1) Expose some variables for this.

```
[SerializeField]
private float maxDistanceForCenterReward = 5;    🌣 "3.42"
[SerializeField]
private float centerDistanceReward = 0.05f;    🌣 Changed in 2 assets
[SerializeField]
private float rewardPerStep = 0.05f;    🌣 "0.01"


            private float distanceToCenter;
            private float distanceToCenterPercentage;
```

19.2) For this, in the OnActionReceived method, add a reward per step. I would suggest a very low value for this.

Then, to ensure that our agent eventually learns to favor the center of the environment, reward the agent based on its distance from the center, with being closer granting a larger reward.

This center distance reward should be ridiculously small, or the agent might prioritize this over its primary objective.

```
public override void OnActionReceived(ActionBuffers actionBuffer)
{
    var inputX:float = Mathf.Clamp(value: actionBuffer.ContinuousActions[0], min:-1f, max:1f);
    var inputZ:float = Mathf.Clamp(value: actionBuffer.ContinuousActions[1], min:-1f, max:1f);

    rb.AddForce(x:inputX * acceleration, y:0f, z:inputZ * acceleration, ForceMode.Force);
    AddReward(rewardPerStep);
    AddReward(increment: centerDistanceReward * distanceToCenterPercentage);
}
```

20) Our next step is to create observations for our agent to allow it to see the world.

Here, we will also update the distanceToCenterPercentage field. For this, you should use a few vector observations to describe the state of the agent and then use sensors to give it information about the environment.
For our vector observations, add the following observations:

- **`transform.localPosition`** – Remember to keep your observations in the local space for better results. Tracking our agent's local position in the environment will help it get a sense of positioning.

- **`rigidbody.velocity`** – We can have the agent observe its velocity to have better control when applying new velocities.

- **`distanceToCenterPercentage`** – We can calculate a percentage affected by a fall-off range for our agent's position relative to the center. We can use this value to modify the tiny reward the agent gets for staying near the center of the environment. Allowing the agent to observe this value will enable it to infer a relationship between it and the subtle reward we give it.

- **`distanceToCenter`** – We'll also allow the agent to see the distance to center value directly, which makes it easier for the agent to infer a relationship between velocity, positioning, and distance to the center.

```
public override void CollectObservations(VectorSensor sensor)
{
    sensor.AddObservation(transform.localPosition);
    sensor.AddObservation(rb.velocity);

    distanceToCenter = Vector3.Distance(a:transform.localPosition, b:Vector3.zero);
    distanceToCenterPercentage = distanceToCenter / maxDistanceForCenterReward;
    distanceToCenterPercentage = Mathf.Clamp01(distanceToCenterPercentage);
    distanceToCenterPercentage = 1f - distanceToCenter;
    sensor.AddObservation(distanceToCenter);
    sensor.AddObservation(distanceToCenterPercentage);
}
```

These observations total eight vector observations – three for the local position observation, three for velocity, one for our distance percentage value, and one for our distance to the center. **Remember to update your observation space in BehaviourParameters to eight to reflect these observations correctly – or to whatever value you require if you decide to use different observations.**

21) Give the **BehaviourParameters** a stack size of three for our vector observations, allowing the agent to infer what changes its actions are making. The reason for doing this is that your agent is physics based, and decisions do not immediately result in the full changes to the agent.

Next, we'll add a **GridSensor** to your agent. Let's look at this fantastic component in more detail.

The Grid Sensor

The grid sensor is powerful and valuable for various scenarios. Interestingly, Eidos-Montréal developed the sensor and contributed it to Unity ML-Agents.

They developed the sensor to be able to observe multiple gameobjects without having rendering constraints, thus allowing the studio to train their agents on headless instances – a headless instance being a built Unity game without any rendering support. By doing so, Eidos-Montréal could train its agents significantly faster than with camera-based techniques.

We'll leverage this incredible sensor in our project, as it's a fantastic tool to learn, and I want to expose you to it. I'd also like to remind you that you do NOT have to increment the observation space to account for sensors.

22) Add the grid sensor component (shown in Figure 7-2) to your agent and copy the following fields. I will show you what they do shortly.

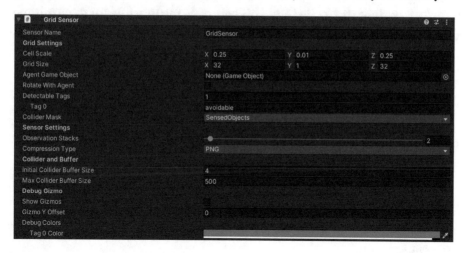

Figure 7-2. *The* GridSensor *component*

The grid sensor works by creating a grid of boxes that are box checked during each observation collection step. **BoxCheck()** allows us to test an area to see if any colliders intersect with a given box in space based on its conditions.

The sensor then collects that data in the form of an image-like structure that feeds into the neural network.

This approach is fantastic as it allows the agent to observe many different objects concurrently without specifying the exact amount of objects to observe.

Let's run through the settings and discuss what they do and what we'll use for the avoidance sample.

Sensor Name

As we learned while building custom sensors, all sensors need to have a unique name on the agent. In our situation, we'll only have a single grid sensor on our agent, so leaving the name as its default is perfect. We also don't typically have a reason to include more than one grid sensor on an agent.

Cell Scale

Next, we have the cell scale. This setting is responsible for determining the size of each cell on the grid. For our purposes, we want an entity to take up no more than **2x2** cells, so we want our cells relatively small – I'll use a value of **0.25f** for the **X** and **Z** axes and leave the **Y** axis scale at **0.01f**.

Grid Size

The next value is our grid size. This setting determines how many cell columns and rows we have, with the **Y** axis value locked at 1. We will use a grid size of **32x32** on our **X** and **Z** axes, respectively.

When choosing a grid size, it's important to know that the larger the grid, the more of a performance impact it will have, both on your training and inference. A grid size of **32x32** still results in **1024 BoxCheck()** calls per observation step.

You should also be aware that this sensor has a minimum size because the sensor internally maps the data to an image-like structure fed into a convolutional neural network.

Depending on your hyperparameter for the **vis_encode_type** setting, which we'll discuss later in the chapter, the following size restrictions apply:

- **simple**: **20x20** (the default **vis_encode_type** setting)

- **nature_cnn**: **36x36**

- **resnet**: 15 x 15

- **match3**: 5x5

- **fully_connected**: No size limit, but you should only use this for very small inputs.

Next, we have the **Agent Game Object** field.

Agent Game Object

This setting should point to the root agent gameobject, and the sensor uses this internally to disambiguate detections with the same tag as the agent. By default, it uses the attached gameobject.

Rotate with Agent

This setting is self-explanatory; it determines if the grid should rotate with the agent; for the avoidables sample, I've set this to **false**.

Detectable Tags

The detectable tags field determines how many and which tags the sensor can detect, excluding the agent gameobject. For the avoidables sample, I've created a tag called "**avoidables**" that I've tagged all avoidable objects with, and I've configured the grid sensor to detect this tag.

You need to configure at least one tag with gameobjects that use this tag for the sensor to do anything.

Next, we have the **Collider Mask** field.

Collider Mask

BoxCheck() calls are quite expensive, but there are ways to optimize this. We can tell the Unity physics engine calls to ignore specific layers for optimization.

So what I've gone and done is moved all avoidable objects onto the **Avoidables** layer.

Then, I configure the grid sensor to only perform checks on the **Avoidables** layer.

The grid sensor defaults to **Nothing** and needs to be assigned for the sensor to do anything.

Next, we have the **Observation Stacks** field.

Observation Stacks

As we've learned, we can stack observations to get a history of those observations.

The grid sensor component defaults to a single stack which shows only the most recent observation. In the avoidables sample, I will use a stack size of **2**. Setting this value to two will allow our agent to infer the velocity of the objects moving through the grid.

Increasing the observation stacks should lead to better-inferred velocity but will significantly impact performance during training time and result in longer training times.

Compression Type

The compression type field in the grid sensor component lets us decide if we want to do any compression on the data.

We will use PNG compression, which is also the default.

Using PNG compression is a free optimization that takes no additional effort and will reduce the data transfer needed between the trainer and the agent.

Not all sensors can benefit from PNG compression, but luckily for us, **GridSensor** can.

Initial Collider Buffer Size

Allocating buffer size is not free, so what we can do is initialize the buffer with a starting size. Keep this value at how many colliders you expect the agent to deal with on average.

For the avoidables sample, I've used a value of **8** as my initial collider buffer size.

This setting precedes our next setting – the **Max Collider Buffer Size**.

Max Collider Buffer Size

Much like the initial collider buffer size, this setting deals with our collision buffer. You want to set the maximum size close to the maximum amount of collisions you expect the sensor to deal with concurrently.

The higher the value, the more memory usage – albeit quite small. I've gone and used a value of **32** for this.

Show Gizmos

Show gizmos is a debug setting we can turn on to visualize the observation grid.

Drawing the observation grid is very expensive and should only be turned on for a single agent during testing. You should turn this off before starting with your training pipeline.

For the avoidables sample, I have turned this on for the primary agent that the camera observes.

Gizmo Y Offset

This setting determines the offset on the **Y** axis at which Unity will draw the observation grid. This setting is purely visual and does not affect training.

Debug Colors

For every tag that you configure in the grid sensor, there will be a debug color that you can change. This setting affects the color of the drawn gizmo that visualizes the observation if you enable the **Show Gizmos** setting.

The grid sensor is fantastic, but I'd like to combine it with another sensor known as the **RayPerceptionSensor**. This decision mainly shows you how it's possible to stack sensors and, as a bonus, gives our agent additional relevant information to observe for training.

Let's take a look at the ray perception sensor next.

The Ray Perception Sensor

The ray perception sensor shoots out several **Spherecast()** calls, which are spheres shot outward and notify the agent of a collision. We can use this to determine which direction the balls are around our agent.

This sensor is also fantastic as it supports a varying number of observations.

23) Add the ray perception sensor component (shown in Figure 7-3) to a child object of your agent.

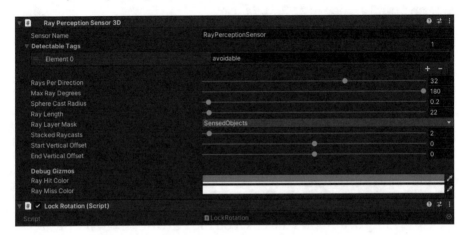

Figure 7-3. The RayPerceptionSensor3D component

24) Attach the **LockRotation** class to your ray perception sensor. This component locks the rotation of the attached gameobject.

```
public class LockRotation : MonoBehaviour
{
    Event function    Dylan "VoidFletcher" Engelbrecht
    void Update()
    {
        transform.rotation = Quaternion.identity;
    }
}
```

This setup provides us with similar functionality to the **Rotate with Agent** field provided on the grid sensor, but will require us to enable child sensors on the **BehaviourParameters** on the agent.

Okay, let's look at the **RayPerceptionSensor3D**!

Sensor Name

Much like before, each sensor requires a unique name on the agent. We will only use a single ray perception sensor, so we can leave this name defaulted to **RayPerceptionSensor** without any issues.

Detectable Tags

The detectable tags field allows us to specify what collisions the sensor should care about when performing sphere casts. I've set this to conform to our grid sensor and used a single tag with a value of **avoidables**.

Rays Per Direction

This value determines how many rays the sensor should shoot out in the sensor's direction. I have used a value of **32** for the avoidables sample.

Max Ray Degrees

Next, we have the max ray degrees field, which determines the arc of the sensor.

Unity appears to have incorrectly implemented this setting, so I have set this value to **180** to surround the agent's horizontal plane with rays fully.

I suspect that this value should be **360** to achieve the same results. Unity may fix this in a later update.

Spherecast Radius

This setting determines the "thickness" of each ray. A higher value leads to less accurate detections but requires fewer rays.

A lower value will result in more accurate detections but require more rays, or the agent may miss some detections.

For the avoidables sample, I found a value of **0.2f** to complement our other settings well. It just takes some tweaking and testing to find good values for this.

Ray Length

The ray length setting determines how far out the rays should be cast. Lowering this can have minor performance improvements, but your main focus should be functionality.

Keep the ray length as low as possible that it needs to achieve the desired goal. If our ray length is too long, our agent may detect avoidables in other training environments.

I found a value of **22f** to work great for the avoidables sample.

Ray Layer Mask

Like the grid sensor, the ray perception sensor implements basic physics optimizations. We can configure which layers should trigger detections.

I've configured the sensor to use the **avoidables** layer for the avoidables sample.

Stacked Raycasts

This setting allows us to stack out observations for the sensor. I've found a value of **2** to be a good balance between training time and performance.

Start and End Vertical Offset

This value affects the **Y** axis offset for the starting point of the rays. Leaving this and the end offset at **0** results in perfectly horizontal rays, exactly what we want.

Ray Hit Color

The ray hit color debug visualization setting simply changes the color of the gizmo when a ray collides with a detectable object.

I have set this to a shade of red for the avoidables sample. It has no impact on training.

Ray Miss Color

Much like the prior setting, this setting changes the color of the gizmo when the ray misses. I have left this value on white for the avoidables sample.

Now that we have observations for our agent, it's time for us to build the training environment, and then we're ready to move on to the training pipeline.

Building the Environment

When building your environment, it's highly beneficial to design it so that it can be copied and pasted multiple times throughout the scene without affecting functionality. Each environment should be a self-enclosed segment.

Environments should also be as light as possible on performance to improve training times.

For the avoidables sample, I want to have the following:

- A floor

- Walls for the avoidables to bounce off of and limit agent movement

- A spawn controller for avoidables in the given environment

- A camera to observe our primary training area

I've gone ahead and configured the environment for us to discuss. **If you are following along from the cloned sample for this book, then you can find a copy of the barebones environment in the following directory:**

`\Assets\Scenes\Avoidance\Prefabs\Training Area - No Logic.prefab\`

Let's take a look at this environment in Figure 7-4.

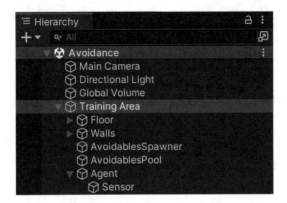

Figure 7-4. *The avoidables sample training area layout in the Unity hierarchy*

For the avoidables sample, I have created a training area gameobject to hold our agent, spawner, and environment.

The agent contains a child gameobject called "sensor" with our ray perception sensor and the rotational locking component.

I have a main camera with orthographic rendering top-down over our primary training area. I have also ensured that the agent's OnEpisodeBegin field is linked to the spawner's ResetSpawning method.

All put together, we have our training environment that can be duplicated multiple times throughout the scene until the performance drops while training. For my hardware, I copy roughly 16 training environments throughout the scene.

Let's see what the training area looks like in Figure 7-5.

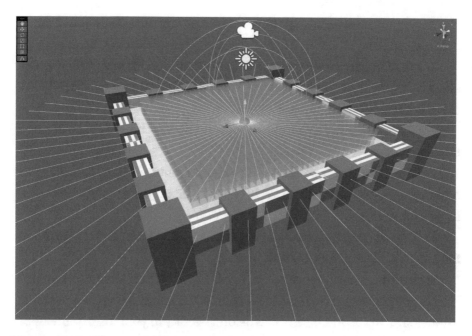

Figure 7-5. *The avoidables sample training area in the Unity scene view*

Once we've validated that we can control our agent through heuristics, avoidables spawning works, and resetting works, we're ready to move on to the training process.

We first need to set up a **config.yaml** file for our trainer to begin the training process.

The config file contains what is known as hyperparameters, and you need to understand these before we can effectively train our agent. Let's take a look at hyperparameters in our next section.

Understanding Hyperparameters

Hyperparameters are often the difference between a competent agent and one that will forever stumble in the dark.

What are hyperparameters, though?

Hyperparameters are explicitly defined parameters that control the training process.

Think of hyperparameters like the configuration for our trainer, which affect nearly every aspect of training – from reward weight to curiosity to checkpoints and summaries.

We'll explore every hyperparameter and discuss how they affect the training process.

It's vital to understand these, but it's also something that isn't an exact science – training can often involve optimizing these parameters to improve your agent.

Let's get started by looking at the configuration file. The configuration file is a **YAML** file and follows **YAML** syntax.

Something to remember is that in **YAML** syntax, tabs are important.

A configuration file can have any name but must end in the **.yaml** file extension. You can enable file extension visibility in your file explorer. Look at Figure 7-6 for guidance.

Figure 7-6. *How to enable file name extensions in your file explorer*

Once enabled, you can create a new text file, which you can rename to have the **.yaml** extension. You can open this file with a text editor or IDE.

The hyperparameters config follows a nested structure. Unity conveys this using the following symbol: →

A → B would then indicate that B is a child of A, with a single tab. In the context of your configuration file, it would look something like the following example:

A:
  B:

The root of our configuration file should contain the keyword **"behaviors:"** which starts our configuration tree. We follow this by our agent name, so **behaviors → agent_name:**.

In the avoidance sample, it would look like this:

behaviors:
  Avoidance:

All arrow notation examples will omit this part of the tree as everything else in the configuration will follow the agent name with at least one indent.

For example, the next step in our tree is trainer_type: which will not be prepended by arrow notation. You must append all settings with a colon. This setting will look like this:

behaviors:
  Avoidance:
    trainer_type: value

Almost all configurations have a default value and can be omitted from the file if you do not want to change it.

Now that you understand the arrow notation, I'll direct you to the ML-Agents page for the trainer configuration file. This page is excellent at describing what each setting does and even provides expected ranges.

You can find the page at the following URL:

`https://github.com/Unity-Technologies/ml-agents/blob/main/`
`docs/Training-Configuration-File.md`

The parameters to give special attention to are

- hyperparameters → batch_size
- hyperparameters → buffer_size
- time_horizon

25) For now, copy the avoidance YAML file from the sample repository:

`\Assets\Scenes\Avoidance\Config\Avoidance.yaml`

The avoidance configuration file will provide a decent starting point for this agent and for various other agents that you might build. Don't be afraid to tweak these values within the recommended ranges, but for now, please stick with the provided configuration.

Our next step is to start training our agent.

Training Your Agent

Now that you're ready to train your agent, we'll look into the training pipeline in greater depth.

1) To start, open your virtual environment, and execute the following command, replacing the values in square brackets with the relevant information, omitting the square brackets but keeping quotation marks:

   `mlagents-learn "[config_file]" --run-id=[save_name]`

   This command will start the training process and prompt you to connect your Unity Editor.

2) Do so by clicking the play button in the Unity Editor. You should start seeing your agent navigating around, and the trainer will post training summaries in your console.
   You're ready to begin scaling your training if this is the case. If not, I'd encourage you to refer back to the samples and book to ensure that your code is functioning correctly.

3) To stop training, select your console and press
control + c.

The first way that we can scale up your training is by duplicating the training zones.

Duplicating Your Training Zones

Duplicating your training zones is as simple as it sounds as long as you've designed your agent and environment to be able to act independently from other training zones.

1) Duplicate the environments, moving them away from each other so that the agents do not touch each other.

2) Occasionally restart your training by using the -- force or --resume arguments following your previous command.

   When restarting your training, ensure that your environment runs at an acceptable framerate.
   You can view the current framerate in the game window by clicking the stats button.
   I suggest aiming to keep your framerate above **30 fps** for physics-based problems and above **15 fps** for nonphysics-based problems.

3) In the avoidance sample, I've duplicated the training zone for **16** training zones – as this is what my Unity instance handles comfortably. Continue duplicating and spacing your environments until your performance nears the abovementioned critical points.

You may have noticed that despite your framerate dropping, you are still not pushing your PC hardware to its limits.

To utilize more of your CPU and RAM, we're able to create builds that can run simultaneously. We will discuss this process shortly, but it's important first to ensure that your training yields positive results.

While you could look at the training summaries, it's better to have our training runs graphed so that we can effectively analyze the impacts that changing our hyperparameters has.

For this, we use a program called TensorBoard.

TensorBoard and Why It's Essential for Training

Staring at summaries and trying to remember the changes we made to our hyperparameters is not an effective way to optimize your agent. That's what we have TensorBoard for, and it's great!

You can access TensorBoard by running the following command in a new virtual environment window:

```
tensorboard --logdir results --port 6006
```

Once you've done that, open a browser of your choice. I will be using Google Chrome for this.

Then navigate to the following URL:

```
http://localhost:6006/
```

Doing this will open the TensorBoard web interface.

Alternatively, I've included a batch file in the Virtual Environment folder of the repository. Simply copy this to your virtual environment folder and run it. This batch file will open your browser and start TensorBoard.

As a limitation, I cannot delay the browser launch until after TensorBoard has finished loading. So you will need to refresh your browser after a few seconds.

Once your TensorBoard is open, you will see all of your past results listed on the left, with your agent's cumulative reward graphed near the center of your screen.

Generally, you're in a good position as long as your agent consistently improves. You also don't want to give up on an agent too quickly either, as sometimes your agent may just need additional time to start making a breakthrough.

We're looking for our agent to eventually plateau at an acceptable reward level for the task.

Give your agent an hour or two of training, or even longer.

This time depends on the complexity of its goal to ensure that your agent is improving sufficiently. If not, tweak your hyperparameters in a new configuration file and rerun the training with a fresh run ID for easy comparison.

Remember to modify your training command to point to the new configuration file!

Another thing to remember is that there is no "right" answer to hyperparameters. It's an iterative process and I encourage you to experiment with them once you have this sample training reliably.

To determine that your agent is consistently improving, you should look for a general upward trend in the graph.

Once you're happy that your agent is training with a consistent improvement, it's time for us to speed up training.

You can see the TensorBoard interface in Figure 7-7.

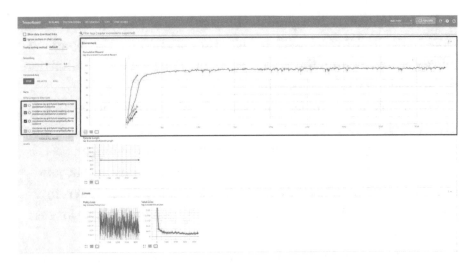

Figure 7-7. *The TensorBoard interface*

Another way to speed up training is by connecting stand-alone builds to our trainer.

Connecting Stand-Alone Builds to Python

To connect stand-alone builds to our trainer, we will need a build.

If our agent does not utilize the camera rendering for training, we can take it further and build a headless build.

In headless builds, Unity strips out a lot of the rendering functionality. This process will allow us to run even more stand-alone builds concurrently without the added workload of rendering.

1) **Open your Unity Hub and navigate to installations. You can right-click your current Unity installation and select Add Modules. Then, select Windows Dedicated Server Build Support and complete the installation.**

2) Restart your Unity, followed by navigating to File ➤ Build Settings.

3) This button will open the build settings window. Select the default scene in the scenes list and click delete.

4) Then drag your Unity scene file into the "**Scenes In Build**" list and click the **Build** button.

5) Unity will now begin compiling your project into a build.

6) Once completed, in your virtual environment window, run the following command without linebreaks:

```
mlagents-learn "[config_path]" --num-envs=6 --
env="[build_exe_path]" --run-id=[save_name]
```

7) Set the **num-envs** argument to however many instances you would like to launch.
    The avoidance sample allocates roughly 3GB of RAM per build that you use for training.

8) Let the training run for some time, as bulk training can occasionally appear slower during the start. Simply monitor your TensorBoard to view your agent's progress.

9) **If your agent is plateauing early, consider multiplying your hyperparameters → buffer_size by the number of environments.**

10) Once your training plateaus are acceptable, you can
     stop the training using **control + c** in your virtual
     environment terminal.

You're ready to export and load your model into your editor for
inference.

Exporting and Loading Your Model

Exporting your trained model is simple.

1) Copy the **omnx** file from your **virtual environment
    results** folder to your Unity **Assets** folder.

2) Then, in the editor, assign your model to your agent.

3) Ensure that you set the agent's mode to either
    Default or **Inference**.

4) You should now be able to click play and watch your
    trained model work its magic.

Conclusion

Well done, you've created your very first ML-Agent from scratch.

In this chapter, we covered the detailed planning steps that you should
take before building an agent. We created our agent and then explored the
grid and ray perception sensors you can use for various use cases.

We then built our training zones and validated that our agent
functioned on heuristics.

You then learned about the many different hyperparameters available
and how to implement them into your configuration file.

Finally, we trained our agent – leveraging TensorBoard for agent
analysis and concurrent headless builds for faster training times.

We wrapped up by exporting and loading our trained model and watched our agent perform its task exceptionally.

ML-Agents take practice and experience to perfect, and it's a journey worth the challenge.

In the next chapter, I'll provide you with a challenge that you can use for practice.

CHAPTER 8

Solve a Challenge with AI

In the previous chapter, you built your first ML-Agent from scratch. In this chapter, I'll provide you with a challenge to solve using ML-Agents.

If you're up to the challenge, this challenge will also have a bonus objective.

Afterward, I'll discuss some extra techniques to consider and touch on how they work and how you can implement them in future challenges that you may face.

The Challenge

We will test your newfound skills now that you've built your first ML-Agent.

For your challenge, I want you to create a small ecosystem consisting of two types of entities. Each environment will feature multiple entities working together and against each other.

These entities can be agents themselves or controlled by an agent brain – whichever approach you find more interesting, as long as the challenge is solved using ML-Agents.

© Dylan Engelbrecht 2023
D. Engelbrecht, *Introduction to Unity ML-Agents*,
https://doi.org/10.1007/978-1-4842-8998-3_8

Grazer Agents

Grazer agents are the foundation of your ecosystem. When two or more grazer agents are in proximity, they should generate a float value called reproduction.

Once the reproduction value reaches a maximum value, the agent should spawn a new grazer agent.

Grazer agents can move around but die after a given amount of time – their lifespan. Their lifespan also decreases faster while moving.

Predator Agents

Next, we have the predator agents.

These agents should hunt down and consume grazer agents.

If a predator agent comes in contact with a grazer agent, the predator should consume the grazer agent – increasing the predator's energy value. When a predator's energy value fills to a maximum value, it spawns a new predator agent.

The energy value of a predator must deplete over time and deplete faster if the agent is moving. If a predator's energy value depletes entirely, you despawn it.

Bonus Objective

We're going to make the bonus objective a bit tricker.

I want you to extend the challenge further to get the bonus objective. I want you to introduce a third agent into your ecosystem.

This third agent must be an agent that a human player can use to consume grazer and predator agents. I will refer to this agent as an hunter agent.

The hunter agent moves at the same rate as the grazer and predator agents but can consume a large amount of energy to "sprint," increasing their movement speed for the duration of the bonus energy consumption.

The hunter agent passively loses energy and must consume grazer or predator agents to replenish energy.

Before You Start

This challenge will be no easy feat, but I know you're ready to take it on.

If you find yourself stuck, remember that you can always open a GitHub issue and ask the community or me for help and advice.

I would also love to see your creation once complete – there is a GitHub issue tag for showcasing your work.

Come and show the community and me what you've made with what you've learned throughout this book.

You can find my solution to this challenge in the following directory:

`Assets\Scenes\Challenge\Ecosystem\`

Additionally, the next section of this chapter will include other techniques to consider when completing this challenge, some of which may help – others being good to know.

Other Techniques to Consider

ML-Agents offer much more than I've shown you during this introductory book.

While we've covered the primary technique in ML-Agents, it's not the end of the road. In this chapter, I'll briefly cover some of the more advanced techniques you can use to train even more advanced agents.

We'll start by touching on CL, also known as curriculum learning.

CL (Curriculum Learning)

Curriculum learning is fantastic for situations where an agent is required to learn several tasks. In our prior RL (reinforcement learning) approaches, an agent needs to accomplish its goal to receive a reward – and from that, the agent learns the association between input, action, and reward.

Suppose you have an agent that needs to navigate through a door to reach its objective, but the door is locked, and the agent first needs to pull a lever to unlock the door.

In reward shaping, if you were to reward the agent for pulling the lever, it might end up training to be highly proficient at pulling the lever and never develop the interest needed to explore beyond the door to get its main reward.

This hyperfocus is the pitfall of reward shaping and where curriculum learning shines.

In curriculum learning, we build environments of increasing difficulty – once an agent learns to master the first stage of difficulty, we move on to the next – this allows our agents to train more generalized knowledge and achieve complex tasks.

We perform curriculum learning by specifying environment parameters within your agent's **config.yaml** file. We can use these environment parameters to dynamically modify our scene or agent at runtime based on its training progress in what are known as curriculums.

Let's look at the structure that we can add to our config file, following the config notation that we learned toward the end of the last chapter:

environment_parameters:

This setting is needed in the root tab to specify that we are now declaring environment parameters.

environment_parameters → [your_variable_name]:

This setting allows us to insert a new key into the environment parameters. Replace the square brackets and **your_variable_name** with whatever you want to use as your key. This setting should be one word and is case sensitive, followed by a colon.

The standard naming convention for this is to use **snake_case**.

environment_parameters → [your_variable_name] → curriculum:

Here, we tell the config that we are creating a curriculum for this environment parameter. All of our curriculum data will be a child of this.

... → curriculum → - name: "[value, ie, "easy"]"

Pay special attention to the dash followed by a space, followed by a name. The dash indicates that this entry is part of a list. This setting allows us to specify a name for the curriculum.

... → curriculum → completion_criteria:

This category allows us to specify the completion settings, determining when the agent will move on to the next curriculum.

... → curriculum → completion_criteria → measure: [reward/ progress]

This setting allows us to choose either **reward** or **progress**. The **reward** parameter allows us to specify a reward threshold the agent needs to reach before progressing.

In contrast, the **progress** setting allows us to specify how long the agent should train before progressing. In most cases, I would suggest using the **reward** measure.

... → curriculum → completion_criteria → behaviour: [agent_ behaviour_name]

This setting allows you to specify which agent this curriculum is for.

... → curriculum → completion_criteria → signal_smoothing: [true/false]

Here, we can specify if smoothing should be applied. This smoothing blends the current reward with the previous reward at a weight of **75:25** to prevent outliers from triggering the next lesson.

... → curriculum → completion_criteria → min_lesson_ length: [value]

This setting allows you to specify the minimum number of steps required for the agent to progress.

... → curriculum → completion_criteria → threshold: [value]

This setting allows you to specify a minimum reward required before the agent can progress.

... → curriculum → value: [float_value]

Here, you can specify the value of your environment parameter at the given step of your curriculum.

Then, in Unity, you can access the current environment parameter by calling the following line of code:

`Academy.Instance.EnvironmentParameters.GetWithDefault(string key, default value);`

It's worth noting that all environment parameters **MUST** be of type **float**.

An example configuration could look something like this:

```
environment_parameters:
  my_environment_parameter:
    curriculum:
      - name: avoidance_1
        completion_criteria:
          measure: progress
          behavior: avoidance
          signal_smoothing: true
          min_lesson_length: 100000
          threshold: 20
        value: 5
      - name: avoidance_2
        completion_criteria:
          measure: progress
          behavior: avoidance
          signal_smoothing: true
          min_lesson_length: 1000000
```

```
        threshold: 60
     value: 8
   - name: avoidance_final
     value: 12
```

It's worth noting that you can also randomize the values of your environment parameters using samplers.

```
environment_parameters:
  agent_speed:
    sampler_type: uniform
    sampler_parameters:
        min_value: 8.5
        max_value: 9.5

  avoidables_to_spawn:
    sampler_type: multirangeuniform
    sampler_parameters:
        intervals: [[3, 8], [14, 16]]

  avoidables_speed:
    sampler_type: gaussian
    sampler_parameters:
        mean: 2.3
        st_dev: .5
```

Uniform

This samples and returns a random number based on the given range, including the max value.

Multirange Uniform

Much like the uniform sampler, the **multirangeuniform** sampler samples and returns a number based on the given range, including the max value. However, this algorithm accepts a list of ranges.

Gaussian

This samples and returns a value calculated based on an average and a given standard deviation.

You should use curriculum learning when your task is too complex for an agent to learn, but you can simplify the goals. The next technique to consider is BC, also known as behavioral cloning.

BC (Behavioral Cloning)

Behavioral cloning is a fascinating approach to ML, but the fascination is not from a pure implementation of behavioral cloning but rather the implementation of BC in conjunction with reinforcement learning.

Behavioral cloning is a technique in which we can record demonstrations for our agents to mimic. However, no matter how much demonstration data you have, the agent will never surpass you.

That's where the combining reinforcement learning and behavioral cloning come in.

The combination of these two techniques allows us to train agents on incredibly complex tasks and will enable them to deviate from our demonstrations to perfect their solution to the problem, surpassing the demonstrations.

Implementing BC is straightforward. Simply attach a **DemonstrationRecorder** component to your agent, set your path, and check the record boolean.

Let's look at Figure 8-1.

Figure 8-1. The **Demonstration Recorder** *component*

The number of steps field optionally allows you to specify a maximum number of steps before the recorder stops **play mode**. You can leave this at **0** to record until you stop the **play mode**.

The general rule of thumb with BC is the more demonstrations you have, the better.

Finally, we must configure our agent to train using the demonstration data. Open your agent configuration and include the following settings:

```
behavioral_cloning:
  demo_path: [Full path to demonstration file or folder]
  strength: [0-1, How strongly to affect the policy, typical
  0.1-0.5]
  steps: [Int value determines the number of steps to keep BC
  active.]
```

When training, your agent now attempts to clone the behavior in the demonstration data to aid with training.

This approach is great for complex environments that you can't simplify. It's best to use it in conjunction with reinforcement learning by keeping the strength lower than **1**.

The next technique to discuss is self-play.

Self-Play

Self-play allows us to easily set up two or more agents to compete against each other. This technique enables agents to train against other agents.

To configure self-play, we need to assign a **team id** to our agent's **behavior parameters**. The team IDs should differ between adversaries.

The next step is to open our agent configuration file and add support for self-play:

```
self_play:
      window: 10
      play_against_latest_model_ratio: 0.5
      save_steps: 20000
      swap_steps: 10000
      team_change: 100000
```

Window

The window integer value defines how many snapshots to store for self-play.

Play Against Latest Model Ratio

The **Play Against Latest Model Ratio** float value defines how often to play against the latest agent snapshot. The typical value for this is **0.5**, but it can depend on the situation. Higher values can result in overfitting.

Save Steps

An integer value defines how often to make a snapshot of the brain that the policy can use for self-play.

Swap Steps

An integer value defines how many steps to wait before swapping the opponent snapshot.

Team Change

An integer value defines how often the learning and opponent teams should switch.

That's all there is to it – your agents will now cycle snapshots between each other to have a single brain learning at a time against variations of previous snapshots.

Self-play is incredibly powerful but can take significantly longer to train, but also typically has more stable learning graphs.

You should use self-play when demonstration data is limited and you want to improve agents against themselves.

I would highly advise exploring self-play when trying to solve the provided challenge.

Tips

- KISS – Keep It Simple Stupid. Whenever building ML-Agents, always start simple so that you can validate that your concepts and foundation are sound. Advanced ML-Agents can take days to train; you want to catch issues as soon as possible.

- Don't give up too early. Watching an agent fumble around can suck, but it may be a few minutes or hours away from a breakthrough. Monitor your TensorBoard, and don't give up too early on training runs.

- Optimize your hyperparameters. Hyperparameters can always be tuned and improved. It's one of the hardest things to get right with ML-Agents. So note your changes and observe the effects they have on training.

- Successful ML-Agents layer multiple techniques together. Don't get in the rut of using a single technique. ML-Agent supports different techniques, so layer them, experiment with the results, and explore the world of machine learning to learn about other techniques.

- Always push yourself to learn more. This tip follows my previous tip; find those techniques, learn them, and apply them.

- Back up your models and checkpoints by using the appropriate config setting, as there is nothing worse than overwriting all of your progress with the **--force** argument.

- If you're using nonrender-based sensors, consider disabling all of the mesh renderers in a scene to get an idea of what your agent sees. This approach can often help with observation problems.

- Use TensorBoard; this is possibly one of the most powerful tools you have at your disposal outside Unity and ML-Agents.

Conclusion

In this chapter, I presented you with a challenge to test the skills you've learned throughout the book. We covered the goals and objectives of the challenge, and I also provided a bonus objective for you.

Afterward, we touched on some fantastic ML-Agent concepts – CL, BC, and self-play – and how to implement these techniques in your project.

Finally, we wrapped up some valuable tips to keep in mind when building ML-Agents.

In the next chapter, I'll cover the path going forward – as you've completed your introduction to ML-Agents, it's time to delve further into machine learning.

CHAPTER 9

Next Steps

In the previous chapter, you solved a complex challenge with machine learning, and we touched on some additional techniques you can use to train your agents.

You've pushed yourself, learning the basics of ML-Agents, and understand what's available.

So, where do you go from here?

To that, I say, be curious and explore.

Explore

The world of machine learning is ever growing, and there are countless ways to apply reinforcement learning and other techniques to solve the world's problems. So explore and constantly hone your mind.

Here are a few ways for you to do just that.

Additional ML-Agent Functionality

ML-Agents has much more to it than what I could cover in a single introductory book; there are many features that ML-Agents offer. Explore the different sensors available to you and build your own.

Don't feel limited by the virtual world; consider exploring interfaces between Unity and the real world. An Arduino, ESP32, or Raspberry Pi project with cameras that stream to Unity and ML-Agents is an exciting way to give your agent the ability to navigate obstacles.

© Dylan Engelbrecht 2023
D. Engelbrecht, *Introduction to Unity ML-Agents*,
https://doi.org/10.1007/978-1-4842-8998-3_9

If you can simulate it, you can train it, and if you can train it, you can make it.

Documentation

ML-Agents also has some of the best documentation and an ever-growing community of enthusiasts and developers. Consider throwing yourself into the documentation and becoming a part of this extraordinary community – perhaps even contributing to the ML-Agents repository.

The documentation can be found on the ML-Agents repository or at the following URL:

```
https://github.com/Unity-Technologies/ml-agents/blob/
release_19_docs/docs/Readme.md
```

You can find the API documentation at the following URL:

```
https://docs.unity3d.com/Packages/com.unity.ml-agents@2.3/
api/Unity.MLAgents.Academy.html
```

Exploring the documentation is a fantastic way of learning what's out there and is an excellent way of identifying what you do not understand.

Always seek to understand, and you will achieve incredible things.

Additional Reading

If you have a thirst for knowledge, there are some incredible books that I can recommend.

Suppose you want to learn how to do machine learning and computer vision with a Raspberry Pi. In that case, the book *Machine Learning with the Raspberry Pi: Experiments with Data and Computer Vision (Technology in Action)* by **Donald J. Norris** is an excellent read.

What you learn here can be modified to feed back into your Unity project with a bit of extra learning.

There will be situations where you need to train an agent on a task so complex that your local hardware will not suffice. In cases like these, you may want to learn how to build ML models on the Google Cloud Platform.

In this case, a fantastic read would be *Building Machine Learning and Deep Learning Models on Google Cloud Platform: A Comprehensive Guide for Beginners* by **Ekaba Bisong**. While the skills that Ekaba teaches you here aren't directly Unity related, many of the skills here can apply to deploying Unity ML-Agents to the cloud for training.

Conclusion

Firstly, I'd like to congratulate you on your excellent progress through this introduction to ML-Agents in Unity.

You've learned so much in this book. You learned about some of the history behind AI and how we got to where we are today.

You also learned the issues we face and the challenges we must overcome to create AI responsibly for the future.

You learned how to set up your virtual environments and install one of my favorite Unity packages – Unity ML-Agents.

You then learned the basics of ML-Agents, and if you were up to the challenge, you even learned how to build your own custom ML-Agent sensor. No easy feat.

Together, we built and trained your first-ever ML-Agent, and you watched your creation stumble into excellency.

You even tried your hand at solving a complex challenge using machine learning, and if you were up to it, you completed the bonus objective and shared your results with the community.

Then we wrapped up some further steps so you're not left in the dark as to where to go next.

Congratulations, and thank you again for supporting the creation of books and sharing knowledge.

I hope you had as much fun working through this book as I had writing it.

The future is in great hands with people like you.

Index

A

ActionBuffers, 99, 122, 123, 146
Actions, 91
   ActionBuffer, 122
   agent policy, 122
   continuous, 123
   discrete, 124, 125
   IActuator, 122
   ML-Agents, 122
   OnActionReceived(), 122
   types, 122
Actions planning, 142, 143
AddForce() method, 145
AddList method, 115, 116
AddObservation method, 107
AddOneHotObservation()
   method, 108
AddReward method, 99,
   100, 126–128
The agent
   Ball3DAgent, 96
   custom implementation, 97
   final view of the world, 104
   MaxStep field, 97
   ML-Agent, 96
   override methods (*see* Agent
     override methods)
   training, 129–133

   connect stand-alone builds
     to Python, 174, 176
   duplicate training zones,
     171, 172
   export and load, 176
   TensorBoard, 172–174
   virtual environment, 170
   view of the world, 103
Agent gameobject, 159
Agent override methods
   Ball 3D Agent, 97
   CollectObservations method, 98
   Initialize method, 98
   OnEpisodeBegin method, 98
   RequestDecision method, 99
   void AddReward(float
     increment), 99
   void EndEpisode(), 100, 101
   void RequestDecision(), 99
   void SetReward(float
     reward), 100
AI-powered robotics, 21
AI road map and classification, 30
   limited memory AI
     systems, 32, 33
   reactive machines, 31
   self-aware, 34–36
   theory of mind, 33, 34

Artificial general intelligence (AGI),
13, 27, 33–35, 45
Artificial intelligence (AI), 1
bias, 26
diverse datasets, 26, 27
game development
BigScience initiative,
16, 17
BLOOM, 16, 17
GitHub copilot, 15
neural state machine,
character-scene
interaction, 16
in games
Chess to *Dota 2*, 14
moral and ethical
implications, 27, 28
traditional software, 28
Artificial superintelligence (ASI),
35, 36, 45
AutoML, 11
Autonomous vehicles, 3, 4
Avoidable objects, 138, 139, 159
AvoidablesAgent, 144
The avoidance sample, 139
actions planning, 142, 143
avoidable objects, 138
config.yaml file, 167
expected challenges, 143
observation plans, 142
reward scheme, 139–141

training area layout, Unity
hierarchy, 166
training area, Unity scene
view, 167

B

Ball 3D Agent, 96, 97
Behavioral cloning (BC)
DemonstrationRecorder
component, 186
ML, 186
play mode, 187
Behavior Name, 89
Behavior parameters, 88, 106,
108, 156
actions field, 91
Behavior Name, 89
behavior types, 92, 93
decision requester, 93, 94
ML-Agent, 89
model, 91, 92
observable attributes, 93
Team Id, 93
use child sensors, 93
Vector Observations, 89–91
Behavior types, 93
default, 92
HeuristicOnly, 92
InferenceOnly, 93
BLOOM, 16, 17

Bonus objective, 180, 181
Brain-Computer Interfaces (BCIs), 23, 24
Brain's reward mechanism, 49
Burst, 92

C

CameraSensor, 121
Card79, 21
Cell scale, 158
The challenge with AI
    behavioral cloning (BC), 186, 187
    bonus objective, 180, 181
    curriculum learning (CL), 182–186
    GitHub issue, 181
    grazer agents, 180
    self-play, 187, 188
    predator agents, 180
    tips, 189, 190
Child sensors, 93
City planning, 5
CollectDiscreteActionMasks(DiscreteActionMasker), 100
Collecting observations, 106, 108
CollectObservations method, 98, 100, 110, 111
CollectObservations(VectorSensor sensor) method, 106
Collider Mask field, 159
Compute Unified Device Architecture (CUDA), 10

Consummatory behavior, 49
Content recommendations, 2, 3
Continuous actions, 91, 101, 123
Copilot, 15
Curriculum learning (CL)
    agent, 182
    agents, 182
    environment
        parameters, 182–185
    Gaussian, 186
    Multirange Uniform, 185
    progress setting, 183
    reward shaping, 182
    uniform, 185

D

DecisionPeriod field, 93, 94
Decision requester, 93, 94
DecisionRequester
    component, 99, 147
Default, 92, 93
DemonstrationRecorder
    component, 186
Detectable tags, 159, 163
Digital mind uploading, 24
Digital twin, 44
Discrete actions, 124, 125, 142
distanceToCenter, 155
distanceToCenterPercentage, 155
Documentation, 192
Dopamine
    in animals, 50
    chemical structure, 48

Dopamine (*cont.*)
    in humans, 48, 50
    in machines, 50–53
    neurotransmitter, 48
    reward system, 48

E

EndEpisode() method, 100
Entertainment, 24, 25
Environment parameters, 182–185
Environments, 165
Extrinsic rewards, 49

F

First ML-Agent
    ActionBuffers, 146
    AddForce() method, 145
    agent's max speed, 144
    avoidable obstacles, 150
    AvoidableObstacle
        Controller, 153
    AvoidablesAgent, 144
    BehaviourParameters, 156
    continuous actions, 145
    ContinuousActions, 146
    create controller, 144
    create observations, 155
    create spawning method, 151
    distanceToCenter, 155
    distanceToCenter
        Percentage, 155
    FailAgent method, 153

FixedUpdate(), 145, 146
GitHub repository, 144
grid sensor, 156–161
Initialize(), 148
local space, 148
OnActionReceived
    method, 154
OnEpisodeBegin(), 148
Random.insideUnitSphere, 148
ray perception sensor, 161–164
ResetSpawning() method, 153
Rigidbody component, 148
rigidbody.velocity, 155
spawner, 150
transform.localPosition, 155
UnityEvent, 153
FixedUpdate() method, 145, 146
Float observation, 105
The Future of AI
    avoid a bad future, 25
    BCIs, 23, 24
    entertainment, 24, 25
    Google, 11, 12
    governance, 22, 23
    healthcare, 21, 22
    IBM, 11
    law and justice, 20
    life extension, 23, 24
    Nvidia, 10
    OpenAI, 13
    Python Software
        Foundation, 9, 10
    taxes, 22, 23
    Tesla, 12, 13

G

Game AI, 41, 42
gameobjects, 96, 101, 107, 147, 157, 159, 162, 166
GetAction(), 100
GetCompressedObservation method, 112, 118, 119
GetCompressionSpec, 112, 119
GetCumulativeReward(), 100
GetName, 112, 120
GetObservations(), 100
GetObservationSpec
    helper methods, 112
    ObservationSpec, 112
    variable length observation spec, 114
    vector observation spec, 113
    visual observation spec, 113, 114
GitHub
    commit, 70
    create GitHub issues, 67–70, 73–75
    open repository, Unity Hub, 72
    pull/fetch, 71
    push, 70
    sample project, 67
GitHub copilot, 15
GitHub Desktop
    clone a repository, 70
    download, 67
    Fetch Origin, 71
    open repository, 69

    permission to open, 69
GitHub repository, 5, 66, 68, 78, 138, 144
Google, 11, 12, 21
Governance, 22, 23
Grazer agents, 180, 181
Grid sensor, 142
    agent gameobject, 159
    BoxCheck(), 157
    cell scale, 158
    Collider Mask field, 159
    component, 157
    compression type, 160
    debug colors, 161
    detectable tags, 159
    gizmo Y Offset, 161
    grid size, 158
    initial collider buffer size, 160
    max collider buffer size, 161
    multiple gameobjects, 157
    Observation Stacks, 160
    rotate with agent, 159
    Sensor Name, 158
    Show gizmos, 161
Grid size, 158
Gym, 44

H

Healthcare, 21, 22
Helper methods
    variable length, 113
    vector, 112
    visual, 113

Heuristics, 92, 99, 100, 126, 146
History of AI
    McCarthy, John, 8
    Minsky, Marvin Lee, 9
    Turing, Alan Mathison, 8
    van Rossum, Guido, 9
Humanity, 4, 5, 19, 21, 23, 25, 26,
        35, 36, 47
Hunter agent, 180, 181
Hyperparameters, 40, 129,
        137, 167–170

I, J, K

Imitation game, 8
Imitation learning, 36, 38, 39, 99, 126
Inference-only behavior, 93
Initialize method, 97, 98
Input data, 104
International Business
        Machines (IBM), 11
Intrinsic rewards, 49–51
ISensor, 106, 110, 111, 118, 121

L

LaMDA AI, 12
Law and justice, 20
LazyInitialize(), 101
Learning environments, 94, 95
    3DBall sample, 94, 95
    gameobject, 96
    SoccerTwos sample, 95, 96
Limited memory AI systems, 32, 33

M

Machine learning (ML), 191–193
    AI, 1
    annual growth rate, 2
    autonomous vehicles, 3, 4
    city planning, 5
    content recommendations, 2, 3
    farms, 4
    "folding", 4
    limitations, 2
    medical drugs, 4
    military, 5
    power and electrical grid
            management, 4
    security, 4
    solve problems, 2
    surveillance, 5
    vaccines, 4
Max collider buffer size, 161
MaxStep field, 97
Medical drugs, 4
ML-Agent components
    behavior parameters (*see*
            Behavior parameters)
    3DBall, 88
ML-Agents
    documentation, 192
    functionality, 191
    installation with samples,
            validation, 83, 84
    sample, 84
    training environment, 51
    training loop, 52, 53

ML-agents unity package setup
   add package by name dialog, 64
   install official ML-Agents
      extensions, 65, 66
   package manager, 63
   Version 2.2.1-exp.1, 64
ML with Unity ML-Agents
   imitation learning, 39
   neuroevolution, 40
   PyTorch, 36
   reinforcement learning, 37, 38
   techniques, 36
Model, 91, 92
Model assignment process, 134
Modern humans, 50

N

Neuralink, 12, 13, 21, 23
Neural state machine, 16
Neuroevolution, 36, 39, 40
Neurotransmitter, 48
Nonrender-based sensors, 190
Nvidia, 10

O

Observable attributes, 93,
      106, 108–110
Observation plans, 142
Observations, 103
   collection, 106–108
   create sensor, 110, 111

observable attributes, 93,
      106, 108–110
Observation space, 108, 109,
      156, 157
Observation Stacks, 160
ObservationWriter, 115
   Add helper method,
      Vectors, 116
   AddList method, 116
   complex types, 115
   index, 115
   observations, 118
   Quaternion type, 118
   simple types, 115
   Vector3, 116
   Vector4, 118
OnActionReceived(), 122, 123,
      145, 154
OnAfterDeserialize(), 101
OnBeforeSerialize(), 101
OnDisable(), 101
OnEnable(), 101
OnEpisodeBegin
      method, 98
OpenAI, 13–15
OpenAI gym, 44

P

Performance-critical projects, 108
Play Against Latest Model
      Ratio, 188
play mode, 187

Power and electrical grid
 management, 4
Precision agriculture, 4
Predator agents, 180
Python, 9, 10, 61
Python setup
 command prompt, 79
 create virtual
  environment, 78–81
 installer, 64-bit Windows, 76
 install ML-Agents and
  dependencies, 81–83
 open command prompt, 79
 Python 3.7.9, 76
 PyTorch, 75
 Windows PATH, 77
Python Software Foundation, 9, 10
Python virtual environment, 130
PyTorch, 10, 36, 75, 81, 82

Q

Quaternion, 90, 104, 118

R

Ray perception sensor, 142
 component, 162
 detectable tags, 163
 LockRotation, 162
 max ray degrees, 163
 ray hit color, 164
 ray layer mask, 164
 ray length, 163
ray miss color, 164
rays per direction, 163
Spherecast(), 161
Spherecast Radius, 163
stacked raycasts, 164
start and end vertical offset, 164
Reactive machines, 31
Reinforcement learning (RL), 1, 37,
 38, 47, 50, 138, 182
RenderTextureSensor, 120, 121
RequestAction(), 101
RequestDecision method, 94, 99
ResetSpawning() method, 153
Reward scheme, 37, 49,
 139–141, 143
Reward shaping, 140, 141, 182
Reward system, 44, 47–50,
 54, 56–58
Rigidbody component, 148
rigidbody.velocity, 155
Robotics, 4, 21, 42, 43, 121
Robust technology, 5

S

ScaleAction(float, float, float), 101
Security, 4–5
Self-aware AI system, 34–35
Self-driving cars, 1, 3, 10–12, 32, 41
Self-play, 187–188
Sensor, 94, 111
 CollectObservations, 111
 GetCompressedObservation
  method, 118

GetCompressionSpec, 119

GetName, 120

GetObservationSpec

 helper methods, 112

 ObservationSpec, 112

 variable length observation

  spec, 114

 vector observation spec, 113

 visual observation spec,

  113, 114

ISensor interface, 111

Reset, 119

SensorComponent, 112

update method, 119

write method (*see*

 Write method)

SensorComponent, 112

SetModel(String, NNModel,

 InferenceDevice), 101

SetReward method, 99, 100, 126, 127

Show gizmos, 161

Space size, 89, 90, 106

SpaceX, 12

Stacked Raycasts, 164

Stacked Vectors, 89, 90

Supercomputer, 11, 17

T

TakeActionsBetweenDecisions, 94

Taxes, 22, 23

Team-based learning, 59

Team-based rewards, 59, 60

Team Id, 93

Tensor, 120

TensorBoard, 137, 172–174, 176, 190

TensorFlow, 10

Tesla, 3, 12, 13

Theory of mind

 AGI, 33, 34

 vs. limited memory AI, 33

Traditional software systems, 4

Training environment, 53

Training reinforcement

  learning agents

 negative reinforcement, 59

 positive reinforcement, 58

 reward system

  challenge, ML-Agents, 54

  create great ML-Agents, 56

  influence training

   time, 57, 58

  ML-Agent, 54–56

 team-based rewards, 59, 60

 training area, 53

 training times, 53

Transformer, 11

transform.localPosition, 155

Turing test, 8

U

Unity ML agents, 40

 package, 36

 practical use cases

  C#, 41

  game AI, 41, 42

  OpenAI gym, 44

Unity ML agents (*cont.*)
  robotics, 42, 43
  self-driving cars, 41
  simulated space, agent
    training, 43, 44
Unity setup
  new project setup, 62, 63
  process, 61
  unity input system package, 63
Update method, 119
UpdateSensors, 119

V

Vaccines, 4
Variable length observation
  spec, 114

Vector observations, 89–91, 106,
    107, 111, 116, 120, 121, 142,
    155, 156
Vector observation spec, 113
Virtual environment, 78–81, 193
Visual observations, 120, 121
Visual observation spec, 113, 114
void AddReward(float
    increment), 99
void EndEpisode(), 100, 101
void RequestDecision(), 99
void SetReward(float reward), 100

W, X, Y, Z

Write method
  ObservationWriter, 115–118

Printed in the United States
by Baker & Taylor Publisher Services